Sam Houston

and the American Southwest

Sam Houston
1793–1863

Sam Houston

and the American Southwest

Randolph B. Campbell

Edited by Oscar Handlin

■ HarperCollins*CollegePublishers*

Executive Editor: Bruce Borland
Text Design: Heidi Fieschko
Production Manager/Assistant: Willie Lane/Sunaina Sehwani
Compositor: KP Company
Printer and Binder: Courier Companies Inc.
Cover Printer: New England Book Components, Inc.

Cover and frontispiece photos courtesy of the Center for American History,
The University of Texas at Austin

Map on page 37 from *Sam Houston's Texas* by Sue Flanagan, copyright ©
1964, by permission of the University of Texas Press.

Sam Houston and the American Southwest

Library of Congress Cataloging-in-Publication Data

Campbell, Randolph B., 1940–
    Sam Houston and the American Southwest / Randolph B. Campbell ;
edited by Oscar Handlin.
       p.   cm. — (Library of American biography)
    Includes bibliographical references and index.
    ISBN 0-06-500688-7
    1. Houston, Sam, 1793–1863.   2. Governors—Texas—Biography.
3. Legislators—United States—Biography.   4. United States.
Congress. Senate—Biography.   5. Texas—History—To 1846.
I. Title.   II. Series: Library of American biography (New York,
N.Y.)
F390.H84C36 1993
976.4′04′092—dc20   92-26949
[B]   CIP

92 93 94 95 9 8 7 6 5 4 3 2 1

For Landon and Clay,
native Texans with roots in Virginia

Contents

Foreword

The right man and the right place intersected at the point at which Sam Houston entered the American Southwest. The encounter made a durable impression on American History.

Houston was restless from early boyhood to old age. He moved about as his family had, unable to strike roots anywhere, unwilling to accept conditions as they were. He therefore long envied the wild liberty of the red men among whom he sometimes lived, and he remained a homeless exile through much of his life. Therein he exemplified an American type that had long fascinated Europeans.

The place in which he would ultimately make his mark was all but empty when he first appeared there. The great Southwest had abundant space, few people—all potential, little actuality. Populated only by scattered bands of roving Indians, it developed but slowly. It existed first under the nominal suzerainty of Spain, then of Mexico after that country attained independence; but it neither enjoyed the benefits nor suffered from the hardships of tight government control, whether from Madrid or Mexico City. Remote from the centers of power, population, and authority, the area lingered underdeveloped. It was therefore open to incursions from the United States of such wanderers as Houston.

The arrival of settlers from the United States, whether authorized or not, created problems that soon led to violence. Disputes sprang from differences in language, religion, outlook, and interests; and the clash of cultures between the remote Mexican government and the heedless, headstrong American settlers ultimately culminated in Texan independence.

But the Texans in due course discovered the difficulty of organizing a stable society within which to enjoy the fruits of their migration. They knew the model of the states they had left and wrestled with the problems of establishing their own government—first as an independent republic, then as a state within the federal Union—while fending off attacks from the Mexican authorities. Sam Houston played a prominent part in these events, first as a military leader, and then as a civilian legislator and executive. In the process he discovered the values of stability and order, so that when the secession crisis came in 1861, he remained loyal to the Union while other Texans chose to join the rebellious Confederacy. His life thus throws light on the development of frontier society.

OSCAR HANDLIN

Preface

Sam Houston forged a life of great adventure, frequent controversy, and lasting achievement. Governor of two states (the only man ever to achieve that distinction), commander in chief of a victorious army, president of an independent republic, and for thirteen years a United States senator, he personified the southwestward march of the American nation during the first half of the nineteenth century. Houston was courageous, sensible, and practical. He was right far more often than he was wrong, and he never hesitated to oppose mass opinion so long as there was a chance of converting it to his way of thinking. In short, Sam Houston's biography aids in understanding the growth of the United States and the possibilities and limitations of leadership in a democratic society. His story both entertains and enlightens.

Many of my fellow historians at Texas colleges and universities must be thanked for their assistance in the preparation of this biography. Alwyn Barr, Walter Buenger, Gregg Cantrell, Cecil Harper, Denise Joseph, Marilyn Rhinehart, A. Ray Stephens, and Ron Tyler all read the manuscript and provided essential critiques. My friends and colleagues, Don Chipman, Richard Lowe, and William Wilson, listened and advised patiently as I worked through the problems of conflicting sources and interpretations. Among my graduate students, Matthew Nall worked as a research assistant and reader, and John Daniels, who completed a master's thesis on Houston in 1991, provided invaluable aid in locating material and arguing key points of evaluation. Robert S. La Forte, chairman of the Department of History at the University of North Texas, offered financial assistance so that I could obtain illustrative materials.

I also owe debts of gratitude to Bruce Borland of HarperCollins for sponsoring my proposal for a Library of American Biography volume on Houston and to Lauren Harp and Michele DiBenedetto for their work in turning the manuscript into a book. Finally, Professor Oscar Handlin did a brilliant job of editing, eliminating more excess verbiage than I care to remember. In sum, the biography benefited greatly from the efforts of many others, but the finished product is solely my responsibility.

RANDOLPH B. CAMPBELL

Sam Houston

and the American Southwest

CHAPTER ONE

"You Shall Hear of Me"

❖
❖

Sam Houston, like Andrew Jackson and John C. Calhoun, was descended from Scotch-Irish migrants who arrived in Pennsylvania during the eighteenth century and moved southwestward down the Shenandoah Valley. However, unlike the Jacksons and Calhouns, who continued on into the South Carolina backcountry, John Houston, who came to Philadelphia in 1730, went only so far as Rockbridge County, Virginia. There, about seven miles from Lexington, he established Timber Ridge Plantation. John's son, Robert, expanded and improved Timber Ridge into one of the finest places in the region. His son, Samuel, inherited the plantation and married Elizabeth Paxton, the daughter of another wealthy Scotch-Irish planter. The Houstons were not Tidewater aristocracy, but they certainly qualified as members of the slaveholding gentry of western Virginia.

Samuel Houston served during the Revolution as a captain in Daniel Morgan's rifle brigade. He enjoyed military life and remained in the Virginia militia after the war, serving as a brigade inspector and attaining the rank of major in 1803. However, Major Houston's modest success came at the price of inattention to his plantation. By 1806, he was on the verge of bankruptcy—with a wife and nine children to support. The fifth child in this family, born on March 2, 1793, was Sam Houston.

Samuel Houston reacted to his financial problems, as did many Americans in similar circumstances, by planning a move to the west. In September 1806, he sold what remained of Timber

Ridge Plantation, paid his debts, and bought 419 acres in eastern Tennessee on which to make a new beginning. Major Houston's health failed, however, and he died late in 1806. His family moved to the southwest without him.

In the spring of 1807, Elizabeth Paxton Houston and her nine children loaded all they owned into two wagons and traveled to their new home near Maryville, Tennessee, south of Knoxville. Although Tennesssee had been in the Union only since 1796, settlement had progressed into the central part of the state by 1807, so the Houstons did not live on a frontier menaced by hostile Indians and lawlessness. On the other hand, eastern Tennessee was thinly populated (the whole state had fewer than 250,000 people then) and largely undeveloped. The Houstons and their slaves, reduced in number to five, had to clear the forests and establish a farm. In the meantime, they lived with relatives already settled in the area.

Sam Houston, who turned 14 the spring his family moved to Tennessee, had little formal education to that point, probably less than one year, but he had spent a lot of time reading the books in his father's library. In Tennessee he proved anything but a dutiful son, showing no interest in school or farm work. He attended an academy in Maryville for a brief period but thought it just as boring as the schools in Virginia. He did, however, discover Alexander Pope's translation of the *Iliad* and found its stories of heroic warfare so thrilling that he committed much of it to memory. He worked at clearing land and establishing a farm, but apparently his effort was indifferent, at least in the eyes of his brothers, who constantly criticized him and complained to his mother. Houston's response was to keep his own counsel and continue as best he could to go his own way.

After two years in their new home, the Houstons acquired an interest in a store in Maryville and decided that Sam would work there as a clerk. Clerking had less appeal than farm work, however, and Houston soon disappeared from his job and from home. Word came that he had crossed the Tennessee River southwest of Maryville and was living with the Cherokee Indians. Elizabeth Houston sent two of her sons to bring the runaway home, but they arrived to find him resting under a tree while reading the *Iliad*.

They were told that he "preferred measuring deer tracks in the forest to tape and calico in a country store." The "wild liberty of the red man," Houston later wrote, "suited his nature far better than the restraints of the white settlements."

Actually, the Cherokees, about whom Houston had heard from white traders in Maryville, were anything but "wild" Indians. For hundreds of years before their first contact with Europeans in the mid-sixteenth century, they had lived in a large area covering eastern Tennessee, western North and South Carolina, northern Georgia, and northern Alabama. Never an especially warlike people, the Cherokees could not match the military strength of the English and colonists in their war from 1759 to 1761, and in one treaty after another they ceded territory to white settlers. Cherokee culture emphasized openness and flexibility, and as a result they adopted the ways of whites more readily than did any other tribe in North America. By the beginning of the nineteenth century, most Cherokees lived as sedentary farmers and hunters in some sixty or seventy loosely formed bands, each with its own chief. Some had intermarried with whites, and it was common to have two names—one Cherokee and one English. The "wigwams" of tribal leaders were likely to be two-story frame houses, and slaveholding was common. After 1821, due to the efforts of Sequoyah, the Cherokees would have their own written language. In short, Sam Houston's Indians were anything but "barbarians" of the warpath and scalping knife.

Houston joined the Cherokee band led by Chief Oo-loo-te-ka (also known as John Jolly), who lived on a small island in the Tennessee River about fifty miles southwest of Maryville. Sam quickly learned their language and participated in their games, hunts, and festivals. He was especially fortunate in that Chief Oo-loo-te-ka liked him and offered to adopt him. Houston received the Indian name Colonneh, which he translated as "The Raven," a symbol of good luck to the Indians.

Life with the Cherokees was, in Houston's words, "greatly to his own satisfaction and comfort," but it shaped his future as well. He developed an abiding understanding and respect for his hosts' culture that he extended to the Indian way of life in general. Few, if any, white leaders matched Houston's concern and sympathy for the Indian. His adoptive father, Chief Oo-loo-te-ka, may have taught lessons that reached beyond Indian culture and Indian-white relations. In Cherokee, the chief's name meant "He Who Puts Away the Drum," signifying a leader who sought conciliation and peace rather than war. Sam Houston would win fame as a soldier, but as a leader, he rarely favored war over peace, even when everyone around him clamored for a fight.

Houston returned to his mother's home in the late summer of 1810 for a brief visit and a new suit of clothes. He stayed long enough to get into trouble by demonstrating a weakness for alcohol that eventually went beyond youthful lack of restraint or the general fondness for liquor on the American frontier. In September 1810, the Maryville militia held a muster, accompanied as usual by tapping kegs of beer and barrels of whiskey. Houston and one of his friends got drunk and decided to beat a drum outside the courthouse window while the Blount County Court was in session. That bit of fun earned him a five-dollar fine for "disorderly, riotously, wantonly . . . annoying the court with the noise of a drum."

Houston returned to the Cherokees until the spring of 1812. In total, he lived among the Cherokees for most of three years. On each trip home, he bought presents such as powder, shot, needles, and blankets for his Indian friends and in the process went $100 into debt with merchants in Maryville. His credit exhausted, Houston had to find a way to make money and pay up. The earning power of a 19-year-old man who had little formal education and no liking for farm labor or clerking seemed very limited, but Houston hit upon a bold expedient—he became a teacher. He opened his school on a farm near Maryville in May 1812, advertising it with a broadside that set tuition at $8 for the term. This was slightly above the usual rate, but Houston indicated that the superior quality of the instruction justified the additional cost. Doubtless the whole venture seemed ludicrous to many around Maryville, but he had to turn away students. When the session ended in November, he had earned enough to pay his debts and found that he thoroughly enjoyed teaching. Later, as a United States senator, he described how, while instructing his students with a sourwood stick pointer as a symbol of "ornament and authority," he "experienced a higher feeling of dignity and self-satisfaction than from any office or honor which I have since held." Sam Houston enjoyed being in command.

The War of 1812 began in June shortly after Houston opened his school. Tennesseeans, Jeffersonian Republicans in the majority, were ready to blame the British for everything from stirring up the Indians against white settlers to threatening the nation's honor, and they supported the war enthusiastically. Men joined the army in numbers presaging Tennessee's nickname, the Volunteer State, earned in a later war. Sam Houston, however, was not among the early volunteers. After completing his first term of teaching in November 1812, he decided to further his own education and enrolled in the local academy to study math. However, Euclid soon defeated him and ended whatever thoughts he may have had of a permanent career as a teacher. On March 24, 1813, a recruiting party for the United States Army came to Maryville, and 20-year-old Sam Houston stepped up to take a silver dollar off the drumhead and enlist. When he went to his mother for permission, she gave it with the warning that her door was always open to the brave but never to a coward. His brothers accused him of disgracing the family by entering the ranks as a private rather than seeking a commission worthy of Samuel Houston's son. Sam replied that honor could be served in the ranks as well as with a commission. "You don't know me now," he said, "but you shall hear of me."

Houston began training with the Seventh Infantry at Knoxville and became a sergeant within a few weeks. In July 1813 his regiment merged with the Thirty-ninth Infantry, and he was offered an ensign's commission. He won another promotion, to third lieutenant (platoon commander), in December. Houston's rapid rise resulted from his learning the drills quickly and from his personal qualities of openness and friendliness. Doubtless his physical size helped too. Always tall for his age, Houston at 20 was 6 foot 2 inches in height and weighed 180 pounds. With wavy brown hair and handsome features, he was a commanding figure who stood ready to live heroically in the tradition of the *Iliad*.

Houston saw action in the War of 1812 only against the Creek Indians, but the campaign in which he was involved offered ample opportunity for glory. The Creeks claimed most of Alabama and resented the constant pressure of white settlers on their lands. Encouraged by a visit from the famed Shawnee chief, Tecumseh, the Creeks in August 1813 began a war by killing 400 men, women, and children at Fort Mims on the Alabama River north of Mobile. The federal government could not respond, but Tennessee sent a militia and volunteer force into Alabama under the command of General Andrew Jackson. Jackson's forces inflicted severe, although indecisive, damage on the Creeks in late 1813. Then, early in 1814, the national government decided to recognize Jackson's success by putting regular army troops under his command. When the Thirty-ninth Infantry marched into Fort Strother in February, Third Lieutenant Houston came under the command of the man who was to become his idol, and at times his protector, for the next 30 years.

The decisive battle in the Creek War came on March 27, 1814, only a few weeks after Houston reached the age of 21. Jackson's army pursued the main force of Indians to the Horseshoe Bend of the Tallapoosa River in east-central Alabama. The Creeks had constructed a breastwork of pine logs across the narrow neck of land opening into approximately a hundred acres of trees and brush enclosed within the horseshoe bend of the river, and they had canoes as a means of escape should their defenses break. Jackson had his Cherokee scouts steal the canoes, opened fire with his artillery, and then ordered a frontal assault on the Creek defenses. The Thirty-ninth Infantry reached the ramparts first, and Major Lemuel P. Montgomery crossed the fortifications, only to be mortally wounded. He was followed immediately by Third Lieutenant Houston, who urged his platoon over the top. An arrow hit Houston in the thigh, but he paid no attention until his men had control of the breastwork. Then, after trying unsuccessfully to remove the arrow himself, he ordered a fellow soldier to pull it out and threatened violence unless he was obeyed. Finally, the arrow came out, bringing flesh with it and forcing Houston to find a surgeon to stop the bleeding. General Jackson came by at that moment and ordered him to stay out of the rest of the battle, but, having promised that Maryville would hear of him, Houston was not content to quit.

Once Jackson's forces broke the Creeks' main defensive line, the fighting became general over the land enclosed by the horseshoe bend. The Indians refused several offers to surrender and resisted to the end, the last survivors fighting from a log fortress built at the bottom of a ravine. Houston volunteered to lead an attack on the fortification and, when his men hesitated, grabbed a musket and ran forward. When he was within 5 yards of the Creek position, the Indians fired, hitting him twice in the right shoulder and rendering his right arm useless. Houston continued to call for his men to charge, but they refused, and he had to drag himself from the ravine where, out of musket range, he collapsed. Jackson then had the Cherokees use flaming arrows to burn out the last Creek warriors and complete a battle that cost the Indians more than 700 dead and broke their power forever. Soon Jackson forced them to sign a treaty giving up their claims to more than three-fifths of Alabama.

Jackson's campaign against the Creeks made him a hero in the southwest, and greater glory awaited at New Orleans in January 1815. But Sam Houston's war was over; indeed, he was fortunate to be alive, for his wounds would have killed most men. The surgeons with Jackson's army bound up the gash in his thigh and removed one musket ball from his shoulder, but they did not bother to remove the other ball, apparently in the belief that he would not survive the night. When he was still alive the next morning, they sent him by litter 60 miles to Fort Williams. The regular army soon continued its campaign, leaving Houston behind with a group of Tennessee volunteers. They took him to one of their field hospitals in eastern Tennessee and in May transported him to his home in Maryville.

Houston began a "tedious" convalescence. In June, he visited a doctor in Knoxville who aided his recovery to the extent that he could travel to Washington in August in search of further medical attention. He arrived in the capital just in time to see the damage done by the invading British army that had taken the city and burned most of the public buildings. The trip aggravated his wounded shoulder, and the medical attention in Washington provided no relief, so he traveled to the area of his childhood at Lexington, Virginia, and remained there until the spring of 1815.

Returning to Maryville and realizing that the end of the war would mean cutbacks in the army, he appealed to Secretary of War James Monroe on March 1, 1815, for permission to remain in the service. His request was granted, and on May 17, Second Lieutenant Houston, his rank attained the previous year after the Battle of Horseshoe Bend, was transferred to the First Infantry and ordered to New Orleans.

In the Crescent City, Houston's medical problems persisted. Doctors reopened the shoulder wound to probe for a bone fragment, an operation that proved unsuccessful and highly debilitating. Following a winter devoted to rest and reading, his condition showed so little improvement that he was ordered to get attention from army doctors in New York. Treatment there helped to the extent that he was given an extended furlough home and then assigned to the Southern Division of the United States Army, commanded by Andrew Jackson and headquartered at Nashville.

Old Hickory admired the courage shown by the young officer at Horseshoe Bend and soon came to respect his good sense and character as well. Houston received a promotion to first lieutenant on May 1, 1817, and, while doing light work in the adjutant general's office, developed a lasting friendship with Old Hickory. Soon Jackson's personal regard for Houston's abilities led to a difficult new assignment that involved the first stages of removal of his old friends, the Cherokee Indians, from their lands in Tennessee and other southeastern states.

As early as the 1770s parties of Cherokees traveled west of the Mississippi River to hunt, and before the turn of the century some began to relocate permanently into what is now northwestern Arkansas and northeastern Oklahoma. Thomas Jefferson encouraged this movement to the west during his presidency with the result that Cherokee migration across the Mississippi increased significantly by 1810. Most of the western Cherokees, under the leadership of Chief Oo-loo-te-ka's older brother, Tallontuske, were traditionalists who wished to preserve older tribal ways and were less willing to adapt to white culture. Houston undoubtedly knew of these voluntary removals to the west but was not involved in any way until 1817. At that point, General Andrew Jackson and Tennessee Governor Joseph McMinn, who also served as a federal agent to secure general removal of the Cherokees, signed a treaty with several chiefs providing for the cession of more than a million acres to the United States and the removal of the Indians to the west. The Cherokee nation was to receive annual payments for ten years, and the chiefs who signed received presents for their cooperation. Trouble quickly developed because some major chiefs, unwilling to give up lands in the east and move across the Mississippi, insisted that those who signed had no power to speak for the whole nation. They charged fraud and raised the threat of resistance by force.

Jackson had his attention fixed on trouble with the Seminoles along the border between Georgia and Spanish Florida and did not want to deal with the Cherokee issue. Therefore, he had Houston appointed federal subagent to the Cherokees on October 28, 1817. Houston returned to Chief Oo-loo-te-ka's island, dressed like an Indian, and used his knowledge of their language and beliefs to convince several bands, including his adoptive father's, to move west. As he carried out this assignment, which he knew arose from probable fraud against the Indians, he insisted that every item promised in the treaty—such as blankets, new rifles, and rations for the trip—be supplied.

Chief Oo-loo-te-ka left for Arkansas in February 1818, but in the meantime Houston's role as Indian subagent took him to Washington, D.C. A delegation of western Cherokees led by Chief Tallontuske came through Tennessee on their way to the capital to protest the failure of the federal government to live up to the terms of treaties made at the time of their removal to the west. General Jackson and Governor McMinn directed Houston to accompany the Indians to Washington to act as an interpreter and, no doubt, to calm their anger. On February 5, 1818, the Cherokees met Secretary of War John C. Calhoun with the young subagent, dressed like the Indians, serving as interpreter. This was Houston's first encounter with the great South Carolinian, and it proved unfortunate. As the interview concluded and the Indians left, Calhoun called Houston aside, reprimanded him sharply for being out of uniform, and refused to listen to the explanation that Indian dress improved an Indian agent's effectiveness.

Houston probably resented being used by the government, even if General Jackson was involved, in removing the Cherokees; he certainly felt slighted by Calhoun. Perhaps he believed that his army career was not making satisfactory progress. In any case, he resigned on March 1, 1818, and then, after accompanying the western Cherokees on their way home as far as Tennessee, resigned as Indian subagent also.

When he turned 25 on March 2, 1818, Sam Houston clearly was no ordinary man. Stubbornly independent and courageous to the extreme, he could stand almost anything except boring routine. However, he had no money and no work and needed a new career. Sam Houston knew how to be exciting, but it was not clear that he could settle down and become a success.

CHAPTER TWO

"A Particular Friend of Mine"

❖
❖

In June 1818, Sam Houston returned to Nashville and began the study of law with Judge James Trimble. Located on the Cumberland River and destined to become the state capital in 1826, Nashville was rapidly developing as the commercial and financial center of Middle Tennessee. As an additional attraction to Houston, Andrew Jackson lived at the Hermitage, a few miles east of town.

Judge Trimble suggested an 18-month course of study to prepare Houston for the bar, but he did not reckon with the memory of a man who could repeat hundreds of lines from the *Iliad*. Within 6 months, Houston learned the standard law texts, *Blackstone's Commentaries* and *Coke on Littleton*, well enough to pass the Tennessee bar examination. And he had time for Nashville's social life as well. Already a member of the Cumberland Masonic Lodge, he participated in the short-lived Dramatic Club of Nashville during the summer of 1818. The amateur thespian enjoyed all his roles except one as a drunken porter in *We Fly by Night*, which called for a red wig and red nose. Sam Houston never wanted to seem ridiculous. He did not object to the use of the absurd if it would help carry his point, but even as an actor he avoided situations that might lead to personal ridicule.

After being admitted to the bar, Houston moved to Lebanon, about thirty miles east of Nashville, and opened a law office. Immediately successful, he used his oratorical abilities to sway juries and courtroom audiences alike and to compensate for any lack of profound legal learning. His popularity grew in both Lebanon and Nashville, and he frequently visited the Hermitage. Through Jackson, Houston became better acquainted with Governor Joseph McMinn and, as a result, received an appointment as adjutant general of the Tennessee militia with the rank of colonel. Then, in October 1819, less than one eventful year after his arrival in Lebanon, voters in the Davidson County judicial district elected him attorney general, and he returned to Nashville.

In spite of his relative youth and limited experience, Houston handled the prosecuting attorney's office well. Apparently the only real difficulty with the job was that it did not pay enough to suit him, so in the fall of 1820 he resigned and remained in Nashville in private practice. Although busy with a successful legal career, he found time to spend with convivial friends at the Nashville tavern, perhaps too much time. A notice in the *Nashville Whig* of December 26, 1821, included the rather cryptic message that Houston, having moved to a new office, "can be found at all times where he ought to be." He also spent time with militia officers who in the fall of 1821 elected him major general of the Southern Division of the Tennessee militia.

Houston's rapid rise from 1818 to 1821 and his personal qualities—proven courage, oratorical ability, and a commanding physical presence—made a move into electoral politics virtually inevitable. Voters in the southwest, unable to resist the appeal of Andrew Jackson, could not fail to support his protégé. Houston began his political career as an original supporter of Old Hickory, a member with Senator John Eaton, Governor Joseph McMinn, William Carroll, and others, of the "Nashville Junto" that directed Jackson's first presidential nomination. Realizing that the caucus of Republican party leaders in Washington would not support their man for the presidency in 1824, the Tennesseeans condemned the caucus system of nomination as undemocratic and had the state legislature put Jackson's name before the people during the summer of 1822.

Houston, as a prominent member of the Jackson movement, found his own political career advancing rapidly as well. In 1823 he ran for the United States House of Representatives from the Ninth Tennessee District. No one opposed him. Elected in August

1823, at the age of 30, he went to Washington that December with a letter of introduction from Jackson to Thomas Jefferson, the patron saint of their party. The new congressman, Jackson wrote, is "a particular friend of mine" who has attained his present standing "without the intrinsic advantages of fortune or education."

Houston spent his first session in Congress studying the legislative process and observing the dominant men of the House of Representatives such as Henry Clay and Daniel Webster. His first speech, in January 1824, was an appeal for recognition of the independence of the Greeks from Turkish domination, a subject likely to attract the attention of someone with a romantic admiration for heroic struggles. On a more practical basis, Houston learned to do favors for his constituents and used every opportunity to support Jackson's presidential candidacy. At the end of the session, he returned to Nashville, where he resumed his law practice and campaigned for Jackson during the interval before Congress assembled again in December 1824.

Houston also became involved during 1824 in a serious love affair shrouded in mystery as was typical of his romances. Several letters indicate, however, that the object of his affections was a Miss M___ from South Carolina and that he expected to be married in the spring of 1825.

Houston returned to Washington in December 1824 to attend an interesting session of Congress. The electoral college vote in the recent presidential election was so divided by the four Republican candidates—Jackson (99 votes), John Quincy Adams (84), William Crawford (41), and Henry Clay (37)—that no one received a majority. According to the Constitution, the House of Representatives had to choose the president from among the three candidates receiving the largest number of votes. Clay could not be president, but as a very powerful Speaker of the House, he held the key to deciding the eventual winner. Houston supported Jackson, of course, and was undoubtedly disappointed when Clay threw his support to Adams and then became the new president's secretary of state. The Kentuckian had several good reasons—agreement on the need for a protective tariff and the Second Bank of the United States, for example—for choosing

Adams over Jackson, whose positions on the issues were deliberately vague or unknown. But Jackson and his friends cried "Bargain and Corruption" and set out upon a four-year campaign to win for "the Nation's Hero and the People's Friend" what the corrupt politicians in Washington had stolen from him. Houston was not one of the leaders in charging that a corrupt deal had robbed Jackson of the executive office, but he remained heavily involved in building the Jacksonian political alliance that soon became known as the Democratic Republicans and then simply as the Democratic party.

Houston's quest for a bride ended as unsuccessfully as Jackson's 1824 campaign for the presidency. Once the congressional session ended in March 1825, he went, as planned, to South Carolina, but something delayed and then ended his matrimonial plans. He explained to a cousin that he would be busy campaigning for reelection in Tennessee and would not want to leave his wife alone and closed with a cryptic comment about "personal difficulties" at home. In any case, he returned to Nashville, did not go back to South Carolina as he had promised, and continued the single life.

Houston's service in the House of Representatives from 1823 to 1825, although not distinguished in any way, was adequate for a first-term congressman. His constituents reelected him without serious opposition in the summer of 1825. All was not smooth, however, because Houston was learning that a man who associated with Andrew Jackson and spoke his mind on political and social issues in the southwest was likely to become well acquainted with controversy. In March 1826, at Jackson's request, he proposed that John P. Erwin, Henry Clay's son-in-law, be replaced as postmaster at Nashville and told the House that Erwin was an eavesdropper and a man of questionable character. The proposed removal did not occur, but it assured Houston of a hostile welcome home when Congress adjourned in August. Erwin, or someone interested in the dispute, brought in a professional duelist from Missouri—who called himself "John Smith T."—to challenge Houston. Houston rejected the offer on the grounds that "Smith T." was not a Tennessee resident and not truly interested in the affair, but then a Nashville lawyer, William

A. White, took up the matter and challenged him. Houston reluctantly agreed to the duel, chose to fight with pistols, and spent a week practicing under the guidance of Andrew Jackson, a man of experience in affairs of honor, having killed Charles Dickinson in 1806. The Houston-White duel took place in Kentucky, just across the Tennessee state line, on September 22, 1826. At the command to fire, Houston shot his opponent through the body without being hit himself. Fortunately, especially since the two men had no real quarrel with each other, White recovered. Houston, apparently disgusted at the whole affair, avoided duels for the rest of his life, an accomplishment that did not come easily.

Houston, like most Jacksonians, used the Congress that met from 1825 to 1827 as a forum for Old Hickory's next presidential campaign rather than as a legislative arena. In February 1826, for example, he made a speech in opposition to sending delegates to the Panama Congress, an early effort at building Pan-American cooperation and commercial ties that Adams and Clay had endorsed. Houston also ridiculed Massachusetts for refusing to allow its militia to leave the state during the War of 1812 and then asking for federal pay for the same troops. Although this speech was partisan in that Massachusetts was the home of President Adams, it was also notable for its emphasis on upholding the Union and the Constitution.

When Houston's second term in Congress ended in March 1827, he returned to Tennessee and ran for governor. This candidacy resulted in part from Jackson's need to assure strong control of his own state. William Carroll had held the governor's office for the constitutionally permitted three terms, and the candidate most likely to replace him was Newton Cannon, a Whig from eastern Tennessee who made an issue there of the recent relocation of the capital from Knoxville to Nashville, a move that Jackson had supported. Thus, Houston entered the race partly as Old Hickory's man, but he also sought the governorship simply because he wanted it and was popular enough to win. Houston seemingly enjoyed his time as a legislator, but like Jackson, he had more the temperament of the executive. He could engage in the patience-trying give and take of legislation, but he preferred the executive's responsibilities of formulating policies and exercising leadership.

Houston campaigned across the state during the summer of 1827, attending political rallies, barbecues, and any event at which voters gathered. Always an effective stump speaker, he doubtless excited his listeners with Jacksonian rhetoric about government by the people and opposition to special privilege. Also, during this campaign, Houston began to indulge a taste for spectacular combinations of clothing, a characteristic that marked him for the rest of his life. According to one observer, he wore a "shining black patent leather military . . . cravat, incased by a standing collar, ruffled shirt, black satin vest, shining black silk pants . . . a gorgeous, red-ground, many colored Indian hunting-shirt, fastened at the waist by a huge red . . . sash, covered with fancy beadwork, with an immense silver buckle, embroidered silk stockings, and pumps with large silver buckles. . . ." All this was topped off by a tall black beaver hat. It may be difficult to imagine such a costume, but apparently the voters of Tennessee liked it. In early September he defeated Cannon by more than 11,000 votes in a total of more than 75,000 and won the governor-ship. He ran well in all parts of the state, showing that his victory depended at least as much on his personal appeal as on the Jacksonian machine.

Houston's inaugural address on October 1, 1827, emphasized his obligation to support the United States Constitution and at the same time to protect the state constitution against infringement by the federal government. Such statements were typical of Jacksonians, and where the line would be drawn between na-tional and state power was by no means clear at the time. Soon, however, Jackson showed that he would permit no state to threaten the Union, and Houston, if he had not done so already, took that message to heart.

The new governor's first message to the Tennessee legisla-ture, two weeks after his inauguration, took a decidedly practical look at the state's condition and prospects for the future. Arguing that transportation improvements were critical, he suggested a statewide plan of development with particular attention to a canal that would bypass Muscle Shoals on the Tennessee River and permit commerce to flow from the east to the Ohio River. He also recommended that the state promote land policies aimed not at forcing prices to the highest limit possible but instead at allowing all individuals to acquire a homestead. Finally, he praised the beginning Tennessee had made in creating a permanent fund to support public schools, concluding that in the future "No longer will the means of elementary learning be limited to those whose private resources are equal to the expense, but the road to distinction in every department of science and moral excellency, will be equally open to all the youth of our country whose ambition may urge them on. . . ."

Houston's dreams of internal improvements reached beyond contemporary technology and the financial resources of Tennessee in that era, but he saw to other important matters such as inspecting all state banks and ran his administration on the basis of sound fiscal principles. His popularity grew to the point that it alarmed ex-governor William Carroll, who had planned to leave office for only one term, as the constitution required, and then return. The new governor, whose approach was so practical and popular, might decide that he wanted a second term.

Houston had no intention of stepping aside for Carroll, but he had another campaign to wage before turning to his own. Immediately after the election of 1824, the Jacksonian Democrats had begun work to unseat John Quincy Adams and win for the Hero what they believed the politicians in Washington had stolen from him. Their efforts increased as the election year approached. Governor Houston helped entertain Jackson at a public dinner at the Nashville Inn during Christmas 1827, and then accompanied him and most of the other Jacksonian leaders on a "nonpolitical" trip to New Orleans to celebrate the anniversary of the great victory in 1815. While Jackson made speeches to the crowds gathered along the way, Houston talked politics with his Tennessee friends, probably telling them how much he disliked having John C. Calhoun as the vice presidential candidate on the Democratic ticket. The run-in with Calhoun back in 1818 still rankled, not just because Houston had been insulted, but because it indicated a basic difference between the two men. Calhoun tended to value form over practicality whereas Houston was always inclined to concentrate on practical results.

Back in Nashville following the New Orleans trip, Houston

continued until the fall of 1828 as an unofficial campaign manager for Old Hickory, a job made difficult by the highly personal nature of the contest. No story about Jackson was too outrageous for public circulation. He was depicted as a bloodthirsty killer who had wantonly ordered the deaths of innocent boys in the Tennessee militia during the War of 1812. His mother, one newspaperman said, was a black prostitute brought to America by British soldiers during the American Revolution. And, of course, all the slanders concerning his marriage to Rachel Robards Jackson before she had been properly divorced by her first husband were revived in new and more vicious forms. The Jacksonian Democrats returned blow for blow, even accusing Adams— when he had been minister to Russia—of having procured a 13-year-old American girl for the evil pleasures of the czar. Houston probably needed no training in the art of political vituperation, but if he did, the campaign of 1828 gave him experience that would be useful in many of his own contests in the future.

The election resulted in vindication for Jackson, at least in the eyes of Democrats, as he and Calhoun overwhelmed Adams and Richard Rush, the National Republican candidates, by an electoral vote of 178 to 83. Victory celebrations stopped, however, in December, when Rachel Jackson suddenly died. Old Hickory insisted that the slanderous accusations of the recent campaign killed her, but in fact while preparing for the move to Washington, she caught a cold that turned into a fatal attack of pleurisy. Houston served as chief pallbearer at her funeral at the Hermitage on Christmas Eve, 1828.

On January 18, 1829, when Andrew Jackson boarded a steamboat at Nashville to begin his journey to Washington, Sam Houston became the leader of the new administration's forces in Tennessee. He planned to announce his candidacy for reelection within a few weeks, and with Old Hickory's blessing, there was every reason to believe that he could defeat former governor William Carroll's challenge. Houston also had plans for what he likely regarded as an even more momentous event—finally, he was to marry.

Eliza Allen, Houston's fiancée, was the daughter of John

Allen, a wealthy planter who lived near Gallatin in Sumner County, about 30 miles from Nashville. Houston had been a regular visitor at the Allen family's home since being introduced there in 1824 by Robert Allen, a fellow congressman and John Allen's younger brother. Eliza was only 15 at the time, a blonde with blue-gray eyes who was a student at the local academy. By 1828 Eliza was no longer a schoolgirl, and Houston, ever appreciative of attractive women, was making more frequent visits to Gallatin. The difference in their ages—he was 35 in March of that year, and she would be 20 in December—did not concern him. He expressed his interest in Eliza to John Allen and received encouragement. The courtship still faced one problem; Eliza did not love Houston and may have been in love with another man. Her family, however—delighted by the prospects of a match between their daughter and a man who was already governor and had an excellent chance to become president—pressured her to be more responsive to Houston. Bowing to their wishes, she accepted his proposal in October 1828, and the engagement announcement followed soon after.

Sam Houston and Eliza Allen exchanged wedding vows before Dr. William Hume, pastor of the Nashville Presbyterian Church, at the Allen home on January 22, 1829. Except for the difference in ages, the match could hardly have seemed more perfect. The couple spent a few days traveling in leisurely fashion back to the capital and then, since Tennessee had no governor's mansion, took up residence at the Nashville Inn. Numerous dinners and receptions followed as local society took the new first family of Tennessee to its heart.

Four days before the wedding, Carroll had announced his candidacy for the governorship; Houston responded with a declaration of his own that appeared in Nashville newspapers in late January. The contest between the ex-governor and the incumbent, both of whom had risen in Tennessee politics as Jacksonian Democrats, promised entertainment to voters across the state, but Houston had great personal popularity and the support, if necessary, of Old Hickory. Surely, it seemed, he would win reelection and continue the pattern of unbroken success that had marked his career since his arrival in Nashville in 1818.

Less than three months after his marriage, as he campaigned for reelection, Sam Houston's world fell apart. Eliza Allen Houston left him and went home to her family. Why this happened, why the marriage failed, will never be known with certainty. The earliest acknowledgment on Houston's part of a problem between the couple came on April 9, 1829, in a letter to Eliza's father. Obviously troubled to the point of near incoherence, he wrote of a "most unpleasant & unhappy circumstance . . . in the family" that had now been settled and that he wished had never come to the attention of his father- and mother-in-law. He referred several times to being satisfied about Eliza's "virtue," without making clear the basis for his concern in the first place, and then concluded with the following: "She was cold to me, & I thought did not love me. She owns that such was one cause of my unhappiness. You can judge how unhappy I was to think I was united to a woman that did not love me. This time is now past, & my future happiness can only exist in the assurance that Eliza & myself can be happy & that Mrs. Allen & you can forget the past. . . ."

Houston, believing (or hoping) that the matter was settled, continued his campaign by meeting Carroll in debate on Saturday, April 11, at Cockrell Springs. Eliza, however, went home to her family, probably on that same day. Congressman Davy Crockett wrote on the eighteenth, that "a circumstance tooke place last Saturday which created much excitement Our Governor Houston has parted with his wife. . . ." The separation proved a godsend to former-governor Carroll's campaign and to those who simply liked gossip. "There is a thousand tails a float," one woman wrote. "He has a good menny enimies and a great menny friends." Houston stayed in his room at the Nashville Inn, visited only by close friends from time to time, and refused to offer any explanation of the separation. Ever the gallant, he never wavered in his refusal, as he put it, "to take up arms against a woman." The crowd outside the inn grew uglier and posted placards accusing the governor of cowardice. He and a few friends walked into the town square, but no one accepted this dare. Had anyone attacked, he said later, "the streets of Nashville would have flowed with blood."

Angry, hurt, and confused, Houston reached out in several directions as the controversy grew after April 11. He asked Dr. William Hume, the minister who had performed his marriage, to receive him into the church but was refused. Reverend Hume may have believed that Houston's faith did not merit baptism, or perhaps he did not wish to offend the Allen family. Then, probably on April 15, the date that he used later as that of his final separation from Eliza, Houston made one last effort at reconciliation. He rode to Gallatin and, according to Allen family tradition, knelt before his wife and in tears begged her to return to Nashville with him. She would not.

On the sixteenth, Houston resigned as governor of Tennessee. His letter of resignation had all the coherence and dignity that his appeal to John Allen on April 9 had lacked. "That veneration of public opinion by which I have measured every act of my official life," he wrote, "has taught me to hold no delegated power which would not daily be renewed by my constituents. . . ." So, although he had a "perfect consciousness of undiminished claim to the confidence & support" of the people of the state, he was "delicately circumstanced" and "overwhelmed by sudden calamities" in such a way that his authority was in question and he had no choice but to resign. The whole, he wrote, resulted from his own misfortune, more than the "fault or contrivance" of any other person. Obviously, the resignation also ended his campaign for reelection.

Houston never sought to explain or justify the separation from Eliza, who remained in Tennessee, remarried in 1840, and died in 1861. She, in turn, said nothing on the matter for the rest of her life. Both showed some interest in the life of the other over the years, but neither ever made, or permitted to be made in their presence, a negative remark about the other. Thus the cause of the breakup of Sam Houston's marriage to Eliza Allen will never be known. The most reasonable explanation is that she did not love him but was encouraged by her family into what they regarded as a promising match. When he discovered his wife's feelings, Houston, momentarily at least, lost his temper, and then, in spite of his efforts to save the marriage, she went home to her family.

Houston stayed in Nashville for a week after his resignation, and then on April 23, 1829, boarded the steam packet *Red Rover* and went, in his words, "to the wigwam of his adopted father, the chief of the Cherokees, in Arkansas." Walking from the inn to the wharf, he wore old clothes and an Indian blanket. As the Reverend Dr. Hume, who had refused to baptize Houston, observed, "*Sic Transit Gloria Mundi*. Oh, what a fall for a major general, a member of Congress, and a Governor of so respectable a state as Tennessee." When Houston left Nashville that spring day, it certainly appeared that glory had been fleeting for him; that the events of a few weeks had ruined his brilliantly promising career beyond all salvation. He had failed to strike roots in Tennessee.

CHAPTER THREE

"A Voluntary Exile"

❖
❖

Houston's only companion when he left Nashville on April 23, 1829, was one H. Haralson, a frontier drifter of Irish descent whose chief known accomplishment was the ability to consume great quantities of whiskey. They traveled down the Cumberland River to the Ohio and thence to Cairo, Illinois, on the Mississippi. At Cairo, the "voluntary exile," as Houston later called himself, and his new friend bought a flatboat, stocked it with provisions, hired a boatman and a young free black man, and set off drifting south. Upon reaching the mouth of the Arkansas River, he and Haralson sold the flatboat and boarded a steamboat to travel upriver, reaching Little Rock on May 8. A young Virginian who saw him there wrote that Houston conversed "cheerfully" and indicated that after spending the winter with the Cherokees he hoped to go to the Rocky Mountains and on to visit Oregon and California.

If Houston seemed cheerful in public, he relied on his skills as an actor, for in a letter to President Andrew Jackson on May 11, he referred to himself as "the most unhappy man now living." "What am I?" he exclaimed, "an Exile from my home; and my country, a houseless unshelter'd wanderer, among the Indians! Who has met, or who has sustained, such sad and unexpected reverses? Yet I am myself, and will remain, the proud and honest man!" He promised to inform Jackson of any matters of importance to his administration, especially in relation to the Indians. Houston closed by saying that he planned to leave in two hours for the home of Chief Oo-loo-te-ka and that letters could be sent to him at the Cherokee Agency.

Leaving Little Rock on horseback, Houston and Haralson rode up the Arkansas until they overtook a steamboat, the *Facility*, which the former governor boarded while his companion continued overland. Struggling against the typical hazards of travel on southwestern rivers, the small boat worked its way past Fort Smith and finally landed Houston at the mouth of the Illinois River, a few miles from Chief Oo-loo-te-ka's home. Word of Houston's coming had preceded him, and although it was night, the chief and his family waited at the landing. His adoptive father offered a warm and even inspiring welcome, saying that the dark cloud that had fallen across the path of his son was in reality a blessing to the Cherokees, for they were in great trouble and now had someone to give them counsel and convey their sorrows to President Jackson. Houston lay down to sleep that night "like a weary wanderer returned at last to his father's house."

Chief Oo-loo-te-ka's band of Cherokees had indeed lived a troubled life since moving to the west in 1818. They had settled first in northeastern Arkansas, only to find that they had moved into the hunting grounds of the Osage Indians and that, to make matters worse, whites were beginning to arrive in the area. In May 1828, a delegation from the western Cherokee nation signed yet another treaty with the United States by which they agreed to move out of Arkansas into east-central Oklahoma. Many chiefs, including Oo-loo-te-ka, opposed this new cession of tribal lands that would necessitate another move to new homes, but the United States Senate ratified the treaty, and there was no choice except to go. When Houston arrived in the spring of 1829, tribal leaders such as his adoptive father were well established with large homes, fields cultivated by slaves, and sizable herds of cattle. Many were not so well-to-do, however, and all were concerned that the whites might force them off their land again. Moreover, in spite of the presence of Fort Gibson, a U.S. Army post established on the Grand River in 1824 to maintain peace in the region, they still faced problems with the Osages and with other southeastern Indians such as the Creeks, who were being moved into the area as well.

Immediately upon his arrival, Houston dressed like a Chero-kee and began to work as an advisor and diplomat for the Indians. At the invitation of Auguste Pierre Chouteau, operator of the main trading post in Osage country, he rode 100 miles farther west into the territory of the Cherokees' oldest enemy. Chouteau took him to the Osage agency and let him hear the Indians' complaints against the government agent there. Houston then visited Fort Gibson, where he met a delegation of Creek Indians who had come to complain about the behavior of their agent, accusing him of profiteering on the sale of necessities and of trying to sell liquor to their tribe. Returning to the Cherokee settlements, he attended a grand council of chiefs as Oo-loo-te-ka's representative. Much to his distress, some of the younger men urged a war against the Pawnees and Comanches with whom they came in contact while hunting to the west. He wrote to the commander at Fort Gibson, deploring the effect any attack on the "wild Tribes" would have on the frontier, promising to do all that he could to stop it, and criticizing the Cherokee agent for not taking action. Finally, he went down the Arkansas to Fort Smith and visited the Choctaw tribe to learn of their problems with the agent there.

Houston contracted malaria during his summer of traveling among the Indians and spent most of August and part of September 1829 as a very sick man. He wrote Jackson on September 19 that he had not answered a letter recently received from the president because the fever "had well nigh closed the scene of all my mortal cares." Old Hickory's letter suggested that Houston consider becoming a missionary to the Indians or attempting to rebuild a political career in the Arkansas Territory. The exile rejected missionary work because he had no "Evangelical change of heart" and explained that Arkansas politics were too faction-ridden and corrupt. Instead, he wrote, his energies would focus on improving the condition of the Indians and preventing fraud by government agents. He also admitted, however, that political events in the United States continued to interest him far more than he had expected when he went into exile. "It is hard for an old Trooper to forget the note of the Bugle," he wrote. "Having been so actively engaged for years past in politics, it is impossible to lose all interest in them for some time to come, should I remain in my present situation!"

In reality, Houston had not left politics behind. He immediately assumed a role as a diplomat and sympathetic listener to Indian grievances. Then, during the fall of 1829 he deepened that commitment by becoming a citizen of the Cherokee nation and undertaking a mission to Washington on behalf of its members. His Certificate of Citizenship, dated October 21, 1829, indicated that it was given in recognition of his former services and "present disposition" to improve their condition. In December, armed with the rank of ambassador by Chief Oo-loo-te-ka, he and a delegation of Cherokees departed for Washington to inform President Jackson that several Indian agents should be removed and the Treaty of 1828 honored. The Cherokees were especially upset that, although the treaty promised $50,000 in gold for leaving their lands in Arkansas, payment the previous October had been in the form of government certificates of indebtedness. To the Indians, money of any kind was of limited interest, and paper seemed worthless, making them easy targets for white speculators who discounted the certificates for next to nothing. Finally, the western Cherokees feared that their fellow tribesmen still in the East would be removed to the West, a subject under consideration by the Jackson administration, without additional land being provided.

Houston reached Washington in mid-January 1830, causing a stir wherever he went in his Cherokee costume of leather leggings, beaded shirt, a brightly colored cloak often called a "blanket," and a turban. President Jackson received the new ambassador warmly, removing any doubts the exile may have had that he had ruined his position with the most powerful politician in the nation. Houston's mission had some success in that Jackson ordered a survey to clear the Cherokees' title to their new lands and within six months fired the Osage, Creek, and Cherokee agents. However, the president went ahead with plans for relocating the remaining southeastern Indians to the West. After completing his work as ambassador, Houston and John Van Fossen, a New York financier with whom he had become acquainted, submitted bids to the Department of War to supply rations to Indians who were to be removed to the West. Thirteen contractors made bids, but Secretary of War John Eaton, a long-time friend of Houston's, delayed awarding the contract and then rejected all the proposals because the Senate had not yet ratified any of the removal treaties and there was no need for rations. The matter ended at that point in 1830, but it would reappear two years later.

Houston crossed Tennessee as he returned to the western Cherokees, causing just as much commotion as should have been expected. The Carroll faction feared that he would attempt a political comeback, while the Allen family worried that he might seek reconciliation with Eliza or go to the other extreme and file for divorce. John Allen sent his daughter to visit her brother at Carthage, a town about 50 miles to the east of Nashville, and had a committee of Gallatin's leading citizens examine the reasons for the end of Sam and Eliza's marriage. In the process, he gave the committee the letter written by Houston on April 9, 1829, that contained references to Eliza's "virtue." The committee obligingly reported that the former governor had fabricated the issue of "virtue" in order to cover the fact that he was an "infatuated" and wildly jealous husband. Houston was on the way back to the Cherokee nation by the time he saw this report, which angered him anew. His public response remained as always—silence. In private, however, he confided to William B. Lewis, a Tennessee friend, that had Eliza come to him, he would have rejected her. "Tho' the world can never know my situation and may condemn me," he wrote, "God will justify me!" He also sent a letter to Jackson, pointing out that he had not tried to justify the separation even to the president. Honor and rectitude were his only companions, he said. "They are old friends, and will not desert me in time to come."

Once he returned to the Cherokee nation in late spring 1830, Houston built a log house on the Neosho River about 30 miles from Chief Oo-loo-te-ka's home but within easy reach of Fort Gibson. Then, to "Wigwam Neosho," as he called it, he brought a wife, a beautiful woman known by many names but perhaps best called Tiana. The daughter of John Rogers—a wealthy white trader who lived with the Cherokees—and a part-Cherokee mother, Tiana was no more than one-quarter Indian, and marriage to her hardly made Houston the "squaw man" his enemies would later call him. She was a widow; her husband had been David Gentry, a white man from Tennessee who had moved west with the Cherokees and had been killed in a battle with the Osages. The fact that Houston had not divorced Eliza made no difference in the Cherokee nation, so he and Tiana were married according to Indian custom and, as Rogers family tradition has it, in a civil ceremony as well.

To support his household, Houston opened a trader's post at Wigwam Neosho. His supply of goods, which arrived in July 1830, included ten barrels of liquor, ordered, he informed the commander of Fort Gibson, "for my own use and the convenience of my establishment." Not one drop would be sold, he promised, to soldiers or Indians without orders from the commanding officer at the fort or the agents for each tribe. Houston argued that as a citizen of the Cherokee nation he did not have to be licensed to trade there, but eventually—after an appeal to Washington— he had to concede on that point.

The summer of 1830 also found Houston returning to a theme that would occupy him from time to time for the rest of his life— mistreatment of the Indians by government agents. He wrote a series of five articles for the *Arkansas Gazette*, telling Secretary of War John Eaton at the outset: "The innocent will not suffer, the guilty ought not to escape." The first three articles appeared under the name Tah-Lohn-Tus-Ky; the fourth, Standing Bear; and the fifth, Houston's own name. "There is a point of endurance in human suffering," he began the first article, "beyond which submission is meanness, and silence would be worse than base slavishness." He cited case after case in which the Indians had been lied to, cheated with short rations, paid with paper when promised specie, and abused by unscrupulous agents. Such expressions of sympathy for the Indian were decidedly unpopular on the southwestern frontier, and Houston's articles drew viciously personal replies. One critic, also anonymous, called him the "turbaned governor," a fugitive from just indignation in Tennessee, and a man degraded by marriage to an Indian. Houston replied that the critic had disproved none of his charges concerning government agents.

Somehow, in spite of his new wife, trading business, and role as advocate of the Indians, Houston's long-standing weakness for alcohol gained the upper hand during the fall of 1830. He seemed intent on getting to the bottom of his ten barrels of liquor all by himself and, as he put it later, "buried his sorrows in the flowing bowl." The Osages called him Big Drunk, and some say that the Cherokees, although tribal legend denies it, used the same name. In the spring of 1831, he campaigned for a position on the Cherokee Council and lost, probably because of his constant drunkenness. Oral tradition has it that he argued with Chief Oo-loo-te-ka over this defeat and, drunk and angry, hit his adoptive father. When Cherokee men attempted to restrain him, he resisted, and they beat him unconscious. Sam Houston at the age of 38 had reached the nadir of his career.

After an aimless trip back to Nashville in June 1831, Houston received news that his mother was critically ill. He rushed to her home near Maryville, Tennessee, and was there when she died in September. By October 1831 he was back at his home in the Cherokee nation.

In December, Houston, for the second time during his exile, headed for Washington in the company of a delegation of Cherokees, although on this occasion he was merely an advisor rather than an official ambassador. On a steamboat bound for New Orleans he met the famed French tourist Alexis de Tocqueville, who commented in his journal on the ex-governor's poor appearance. After a brief stay in Washington, Houston then went on to New York, where John Van Fossen introduced him to James Prentiss, a financier and major partner in the Galveston Bay and Texas Land Company. Prentiss was heavily involved in speculation in Texas lands, and the two discussed the possibility that Houston might travel to Texas to gather information and survey the situation there. Nothing was settled, however, before he returned to Washington in April and found that the Indian ration contract proposal made back in 1830 had created a serious controversy.

The *National Intelligencer* of April 3, 1832, carried an account of a recent speech by Congressman William Stanbery of Ohio, asking if Secretary of War John Eaton had been "removed in consequence of his attempt fraudulently to give to Governor Houston the contract for Indian rations?" In reality, Eaton, along with Secretary of State Martin Van Buren, had resigned in 1831 as part of the solution to the scandal that developed when the wives of key members of the Jackson administration, led by Mrs. Floride Calhoun, snubbed the secretary of war's wife, Peggy, because of her questionable past. Stanbery, however, used this opportunity to impute fraud to Eaton and Houston as a means of attacking their friend and protector, President Andrew Jackson. Houston immediately wrote to the congressman, asking if the newspaper had reported his remarks correctly, but he received in return only a statement that he had no right to make such a request. Enraged, Houston began to carry a hickory cane cut from a tree at the Hermitage and let it be known that he would punish Stanbery the next time they met. Stanbery, in turn, began to carry a pistol. On the night of April 13, the two met on Pennsylvania Avenue, whereupon Houston hit the congressman with his cane and, when Stanbery tried to get away, jumped on his back and dragged him to the ground. Stanbery tried to use his pistol, but it misfired, and Houston, having his opponent on his back with his feet in the air, proceeded to cane him, in the words of one observer, "elsewhere." When the affair ended, the congressman had a good many bumps and bruises—and a great deal more damage to his dignity.

Stanbery took to his bed and had the story of the attack put before the House of Representatives, which by a vote of 145 to 25 passed a resolution calling for Houston's arrest and punishment. This action rested on highly questionable legal grounds, as Congressman James K. Polk pointed out, but members of the House felt offended, and Jackson's enemies did not want to miss an opportunity to embarrass the administration. Appearing for his "arraignment" on April 17, Houston insisted that he had reacted only to the article in the *Intelligencer,* not to Stanbery's words in the House, and that he had caned the congressman in a fit of anger only after polite requests for an explanation had been refused.

"The accused," he said, "denies that he intended to commit, or that he believed that he was committing, any contempt toward the House of Representatives. . . ." The House decided that he was pleading "not guilty" and gave him two days to prepare his defense.

Houston's trial before the House lasted nearly a month and played to packed galleries throughout. He hired Francis Scott Key, author of "The Star-Spangled Banner," to defend him, but once the prosecution completed its case one week into the trial, Key opened the defense poorly. Jackson demanded that Houston take over his own trial and provided the money necessary for proper dress for the occasion. The defendant cross-examined those who gave testimony for the prosecution, questioned his own witnesses, and finally, on May 7, brought the whole proceeding to a climax with a lengthy speech of summation. In spite of having drunk past midnight on the night before and not being sure that he would even be able to keep down a cup of coffee the next morning, Houston gave a brilliant performance. He again denied that he had shown contempt for Congress and accused Stanbery of slandering him in a public newspaper. For that, he said, "I chastised him as I would a dog." He quoted poetry on the subject of hope for a man of character, no matter how low he had fallen, and he referred to tyrants throughout history. Finally, returning to the argument that the House did not have the power to arrest, prosecute, and judge him, he pointed to the American flag and concluded: "So long as that flag shall bear aloft its glittering stars . . . shall the rights of American citizens be preserved safe and unimpaired, and transmitted as a sacred legacy from one generation to another, till discord shall wreck the spheres . . . and not one fragment of all creation be left to chafe on the bosom of eternity's waves." As he took his seat and the audience applauded, the noted actor, Junius Brutus Booth, said, "Houston, take my laurels!"

The performance won acclaim, but it did not persuade the majority in the House. After four days of debate, Houston was found guilty and sentenced to receive a reprimand from the Speaker of the House, his friend, Andrew Stevenson. The Speaker began by complimenting the culprit's intelligence and character and concluded: "I forbear to say more than to pronounce the judgment of the House, which is that you . . . be reprimanded at the bar by the Speaker, and . . . I do reprimand you accordingly." Congressman Stanbery, not knowing when to quit, then convinced the House to appoint a committee to investigate the charges of fraud on the part of Eaton and Houston. Six weeks of hearings resulted in a split vote for acquittal. In the interval, Stanbery sought unsuccessfully to have Houston excluded forever from the lobby of the House and, successfully, to have him indicted on a charge of criminal assault in the federal court for the District of Columbia. This case finally ended on June 28, 1832, with a conviction and a fine of $500 and costs, but the court gave him a year to pay, and Jackson remitted the fine in 1834. Houston got in the last word on July 10 by publishing a lengthy public letter that defended his motives and conduct throughout and concluded on Stanbery: "His vices are too odious to merit pity, and his spirit too mean to deserve contempt."

Years later Houston insisted that the Stanbery affair rescued him from the obscurity of a drunken exile with the Indians. "I was dying out," he told George W. Paschal, one of his Texas friends, "and had they taken me before a Justice of the Peace and fined me ten dollars for assault and battery, they would have killed me. But they gave me a national tribunal for a theater and set me up again." No doubt Houston enjoyed a greater reputation and renewed self-esteem from occupying center stage in Washington and being in the complete confidence of Andrew Jackson again, but the affair did not "set him up again" in the sense of heading him for Texas. That possibility developed from talks with James Prentiss before Stanbery's remarks were published.

Houston had continued to correspond with Prentiss throughout the months consumed by the Stanbery affair. On April 8, five days before the caning, he informed the New Yorker that if the interests of the Galveston Bay and Texas Land Company required it, he could within a few days "repair to TEXAS" as its agent. "Since I saw you," he added, "I have concluded to visit Texas, at all events this Spring or Summer, but will go [by] way of Nashville." This decision, reached early in 1832, proved very important, because in spite of extensive negotiations that continued even after Houston left Washington in mid-July, he and Prentiss did not reach an agreement. His last letter to the New Yorker, dated September 15, 1832, in Nashville, complained about the loss of two months in trying to make an arrangement with the company. "The matter of Texas, has to my mortification, not turned out, as I had hoped and believed," he wrote, "but I shall 'cast my bread upon the waters, and look for its return after many days.' Tomorrow morning I am to set out for there!"

Although Houston's hopes for representing the Galveston Bay and Texas Land Company fell through, he did not travel to Texas solely for private purposes. Instead, President Jackson requested that he meet with the Comanche Indians, the fearsome lords of the Texas plains, and seek an arrangement that would prevent potential conflict with the southeastern tribes as they were removed to the West. The War Department also asked for information on the numerous tribes of Plains Indians who might act as buffers between the Comanches and new arrivals such as the Cherokees. Houston's passport for this mission, signed by the acting Secretary of War and dated August 6, 1832, requested "all the Tribes of Indians, whether in amity with the UNITED STATES, or as yet not allied to them by Treaties, to permit safely and freely to pass through their respective Territories, General Sam Houston, a Citizen of the UNITED STATES, thirty-eight years of age, six feet, two inches in stature, brown hair, and light complexion; and in case of need, to give him all lawful aid and protection."

Houston left Nashville in mid-September and reached Wigwam Neosho early the next month. While visiting with his Cherokee friends in the area and the whites at Fort Gibson, he prepared to end his exile among the Indians. According to legend, he asked Tiana to go with him to Texas and, when she would not, gave her title to his land, home, and two slaves. This "divorce" completed and farewells said, he rode south from the Cherokee nation through what he called "the least inviting country, that I have ever seen" until he reached Fort Towson on the Red River. From that point, he wrote to Henry L. Ellsworth, the Indian Commissioner at Fort Gibson, reporting on what he knew about the Pawnees and Comanches, explaining that the only way to meet the latter tribe of "wild Indians" was to go to San Antonio, and expressing the hope that a general council of the Plains Indians might be held at Fort Gibson the next spring. He asked Ellsworth to send a copy of his letter to the War Department and explain that another report could not be made until he returned to the United States. On December 2, 1832, Houston crossed the Red River into Texas. It was a moment of destiny, although not even he could imagine the future that lay in the vast expanses of land opening to the southwest before him.

Why did Sam Houston go to Texas in 1832? The ostensible answer is that he went on a mission to the Indians and to examine prospects in general, but as early as 1829 rumor had him planning to lead a revolution to take Texas from Mexico and join it to the United States, and the charge persists that Andrew Jackson sent him across the Red River for that purpose. Such stories made good gossip at the time, and they have made good reading ever since. The only problem is that, although Jackson doubtless wanted Texas, and Houston clearly expressed interest in the province before December 1832, there is no reliable documentary evidence to support charges of a conspiracy to create revolution there. Indeed, available documents suggest anything but a plot. When, for example, Jackson heard rumors in June 1829, shortly after Houston left Tennessee to live with the Cherokees, that the exile planned to use the Indians to conquer Texas, he immediately wrote to condemn "so wild a scheme" and ask for a "pledge of honor" that "you will never engage in any enterprise injurious to your country." Houston had heard the rumors, too, and had already sought to assure Jackson that they were ridiculous. "You have seen my private, & my official acts," he wrote, "to these I *refer* you. To what wou[l]d they all amount, and for what would I live? but for my honor, and the honor and safety of my country? Nothing!"

When he was drinking, Houston talked wildly of many exciting new places, including the Rocky Mountains, California, and Oregon as well as Texas, but he did not have revolution in mind when he crossed the Red River in 1832. The only decision that he had made was to end his exile with the Cherokees and seek financial opportunity and perhaps even a return to public life. How he would attain those ends was very uncertain. He came to Texas not as a revolutionary schemer but as a restless man seeking a new beginning, and he was not positive, even as he entered Texas, that his future lay in that direction.

CHAPTER FOUR

"The Finest Country ... Upon the Globe"

❖
❖

Although the Spanish had mapped the coast as early as 1519, explored much of the interior during the next two centuries, and established permanent missions and presidios after 1715, the Texas that Houston rode into in 1832 had achieved major population growth only in the previous decade. For nearly three hundred years, the government in Madrid largely ignored the far northern reaches of New Spain (Colonial Mexico) unless there was a threat from another nation, usually France. The area that became Texas never had a non-Indian population of more than 5,000 at any time before Mexico gained its independence from Spain in 1821. The only towns of notable size then were Nacogdoches, San Antonio, La Bahía (now Goliad), and Laredo (which under Spanish and Mexican rule was not considered part of Texas). Thus, Anglo-Americans, pushing toward Texas from the east after the United States bought Louisiana in 1803, found the province's rich lands invitingly empty except for Indian residents.

The Adams-Onís Treaty of 1819–1821 established a boundary between the territory acquired by the United States in the Louisiana Purchase and Texas, but only natural barriers, not lines on maps, would slow Anglo settlers moving southwestward. Even before the treaty was completed, they were crossing the Sabine River into East Texas and forming settlements on the south side of the Red River in the northeast. Then, the revolutionary Cortes

Red River

Jonesboro Crossing

Alton · McKinney · Greenville · Daingerfield · Jefferson

Bird's Fort · Gilmer · Marshall
Fort Worth · Dallas · Sabine River

Brazos River · Waxahachie · Trinity River · Tyler · Carthage · Natchitoches
Corsicana · Henderson · Shelbyville
Fairfield · Palestine · Rusk · Nacogdoches
Centerville · San Augustine
Waco · Falls of the Brazos
Belton · Neches River · Aylish Bayou

Colorado River · Raven Hill
Huntsville

Washington-on-the-Brazos · San Jacinto River · Grand Cane
Austin · Bastrop · Independence · Groce's · Liberty
Guadalupe River · Camp West of Brazos · Lynchburg · Sabine
San Marcos · La Grange · San Felipe · Cedar Point
New Braunfels · Seguin · Columbus · Houston
Gonzales · Harrisburg · Galveston Bay
San Antonio · New Washington · Galveston
Columbia

Coleto Creek
Goliad · Victoria

Refugio · Matagorda Bay · Gulf of Mexico

Copano Bay

⊙ Places of Residence

Sam Houston's Texas

(parliament) that began to govern Spain in 1820, wishing to encourage the flow of colonists as a means of developing Mexico's northern frontier, enacted legislation permitting foreigners to settle in Texas so long as they respected the constitution and laws of the government in Madrid. Local officials in San Antonio reacted enthusiastically and recommended in November 1820 that prospective settlers be given land grants on the major rivers in Texas and that the government help protect them against the Indians. Shortly thereafter, Moses Austin, a Connecticut-born entrepreneur who had moved from Virginia to Missouri in 1798 while that area still belonged to Spain, arrived in San Antonio and won approval for a scheme to settle 300 families from the United States as colonists in Texas.

Moses Austin died in June 1821, leaving his colonizing project in the capable hands of his son, Stephen F. Austin, a 27-year-old native of Virginia who had experience in both politics and business in Missouri. The younger Austin immediately traveled to San Antonio, was confirmed as the heir to his father's grant, and went to work publicizing the new colony. Settlers began to arrive and claim land on the lower Brazos and Colorado rivers at the end of 1821. Austin's colony suffered a temporary setback in 1822 when the newly independent government of Mexico refused to recognize the contract granted by Spanish officials, but in January 1823, the recently proclaimed emperor, Agustín de Iturbide, approved a colonization law that permitted settlement to continue. Iturbide was soon overthrown, and Mexico became a federal republic under the Constitution of 1824. At that time, Texas and Coahuila were joined as a single state in the new Mexican union. Leaders in Mexico City thought that Texas, which had traditionally been separated from Coahuila at the Nueces River, did not have the population to merit separate statehood. These changes increased rather than slowed colonization because the central government and the state of Coahuila and Texas soon passed new colonization laws permitting other *empresarios* (colonization agents) to join Austin in the business of settling Anglo-Americans in the region stretching from the Sabine River to the Nueces River. The state Colonization Law of 1825 allowed each family to receive 4,428 acres (a league) for grazing and 177 (a labor) for farming at a cost of approximately $100, due four years after arrival. At that time in the United States, public land sold for $1.25 per acre, payable immediately. As one settler put it later: "What the discovery of gold was to California, the Colonization Act of 1825 was to Texas."

By 1830, two years before Houston arrived, the area between the Sabine and Nueces rivers had a population of approximately 20,000 and was well on its way to becoming an Anglo province within the Mexican nation. Immigrants from the United States got along well enough with many of the Tejanos, Mexicans such as the Seguín family of San Antonio who were native to Texas, but Anglo-Americans also differed in significant ways with the vast majority of the people of Mexico, especially with those who governed in far-distant Mexico City. The languages were different, and Mexican citizenship necessitated joining the Roman Catholic Church, a requirement that the overwhelmingly Protestant Anglos met officially but ignored in belief and practice. Slavery constituted a much more important difference. Fired with revolutionary enthusiasm and never having had an economic stake in it, Mexico during the 1820s regularly threatened to restrict or abolish slavery. Immigrants from the United States, most of whom were from the South, had no liberal qualms about slavery and believed that their "Peculiar Institution" was the only way to provide the labor for cash-crop agriculture in Texas. Mexico's threats proved largely empty, and the national and state governments never did anything effective to restrict or prohibit slavery in Texas. But even their threats worried Anglo immigrants.

Politics also constituted a notable difference between the immigrants and their adopted nation. Mexico did not emerge from its revolution with a consensus concerning political principles and, as a result, suffered highly unstable government for many years. In the 1828 presidential elections, for example, the conservative candidate, Manuel Gómez Pedraza, won over Vicente Guerrero, but liberals rebelled and in 1829, with the aid of a young officer named Antonio López de Santa Anna, made Guerrero president and Anastasio Bustamante vice president. Then, at the beginning of 1830, Bustamante overthrew Guerrero and took the presidency for himself. Anglos generally disliked instability in government, and they would become especially concerned during the early 1830s when these political contests turned on the issue of federalism as represented by the Constitution of 1824 versus centralization of power in Mexico City. Settlers from the United States had a long tradition of opposition to centralized authority.

Finally, to these cultural differences separating the majority of Anglos from most Mexicans, there must be added the matter of ethnic background. Immigrants from the United States generally thought themselves superior to Mexicans, and Sam Houston was no exception. In his first letter to Andrew Jackson after reaching Texas, he wrote that Mexico's rulers were dishonest and her people uneducated. Mexican leaders in turn tended to lump all Anglos as unprincipled land speculators who came to Texas with the intention of stealing it for the United States.

Thus, the peopling of Texas by Anglos during the 1820s laid the groundwork for conflict. Trouble appeared for the first time in 1826 when the so-called Fredonian Rebellion broke out in Nacogdoches. Haden Edwards, an empresario who received a contract in 1825 to settle 800 families in East Texas, created this incident by threatening the land claims of old settlers in the area and by interfering in local elections. Upon receiving complaints about Edwards's actions, the governor of Coahuila and Texas nullified his grant in June 1826, and ordered him to leave Texas. The empresario had already returned to the United States, but his brother, Benjamin Edwards, at the head of thirty or forty men in Nacogdoches, declared independence for the Republic of Fredonia in December 1826. This Fredonian Rebellion did not have the support of most Anglos in Texas; indeed, Stephen F. Austin sent militia to join the troops from San Antonio that put a quick end to the uprising in January 1827. Nevertheless, it aroused suspicion among Mexican authorities about the intentions of Anglo settlers and added to a growing concern in Mexico City that the United States meant to take Texas one way or the other. The Adams administration had indicated that it would like to buy the province. If a purchase proved impossible, the Mexicans reasoned, the Anglos might turn to revolution.

Faced with this threat, President Guadalupe Victoria sent

General Manuel de Mier y Terán on an inspection tour of Texas to report on how best to keep the province loyal to Mexico. Terán spent the first half of 1828 in Texas and compiled a report that reflected both alarm and pessimism. Pointing out that Anglos outnumbered Mexicans by a margin of ten to one, he wrote: "Either the government occupies Texas now, or it is lost forever, for there can be no possibility of reconquest when our base of operations would be three hundred leagues distant while our enemies would be carrying on the struggle close to their base. . . ." He recommended colonizing Mexican nationals and Germans in Texas, basing more troops there, and encouraging coastal trade between Mexico and the province.

Two years after Terán's inspection tour, the Mexican Congress passed the Law of April 6, 1830, a measure intended to keep Texas under control. This law prohibited immigration from the United States, canceled all empresario contracts except those that had already brought in the requisite number of families, and called for the collection of customs duties on imports and exports. The regime of President Anastasio Bustamante then sent additional troops to Texas, built six new forts at strategic positions, and appointed a customs collector. The new law and the accompanying enforcement measures soon led to trouble in East Texas, most notably between settlers and the commander of the new post at Anahuac on the northern shore of Galveston Bay, John Davis Bradburn, a Kentuckian in the service of Mexico. In 1831 Bradburn stopped the granting of land titles to colonists who had been in the area prior to passage of the Law of April 6, 1830, and in the early summer of 1832 arrested two Anglos, William Barrett Travis and Patrick Jack, who had annoyed him with rumors that an armed force from Louisiana intended to take a runaway slave that he had captured. A group of 150 armed colonists demanded that Travis and Jack be released and, when Bradburn refused, sent to Brazoria for cannon to mount an attack on his fort.

As Anglos stood on the verge of opposing Mexican authority with force in June 1832, they gained an important advantage from developments in Mexico City, where General Santa Anna accused President Bustamante of undermining federalism and led a revolt to reinstate the Constitution of 1824. This development allowed colonists in Texas, such as those gathered at Anahuac, to oppose Bradburn and other Bustamante appointees while claiming that they simply supported Santa Anna and the federal constitution. The problem at Anahuac ended without bloodshed when Colonel José de las Piedras, the commander of Mexican troops at Nacogdoches, arrived and, outranking Bradburn and accepting the complaints of local settlers, ordered Travis and Jack released to civil authorities. However, when the men bringing cannon from Brazoria tried to pass the fort at Velasco on the lower Brazos River, the resulting battle took the lives of at least ten Texans and five Mexican soldiers before the garrison surrendered. Also, once Colonel de las Piedras, a Bustamante supporter, returned to Nacogdoches, he was attacked by local settlers and forced to surrender. In both cases the Mexican troops declared for Santa Anna and were allowed to go home. Anglos thus swept East Texas clear of Mexican authority during the summer of 1832, demonstrating how easily trouble could develop between settlers and the government.

The majority did not favor revolution, however. Colonists at San Felipe de Austin, the empresario's base of operations on the Brazos River, called a convention of representatives of all parts of Texas to meet in their town on October 1, 1832. The purpose was to consider the condition of Texas in light of the recent disturbances and to seek reforms made possible, it was hoped, by the overthrow of Bustamante. Fifty-eight delegates attended the convention, elected as chairman Stephen F. Austin, who was known for his loyalty to Mexico, and adopted resolutions supporting the Constitution of 1824. They also asked for repeal of the restriction on immigration from the United States, immunity from customs duties for three years, a school system, and separation of Texas from Coahuila. These requests—especially that for separate statehood in the Mexican federal union— obviously involved major reforms that would have allowed Texas to grow and control to a large extent its own affairs, but they were not revolutionary in nature. Mexican authorities, however, reacted by pointing out that unofficial meetings were illegal and refusing to consider proposals that did not come from duly constituted agencies. The Anglos responded by calling another convention to meet at San Felipe in April 1833, intending to pass similar resolutions and then have the local governing council submit them to Mexico City.

Thus, when Sam Houston crossed the Red River in December 1832, the preconditions for trouble between Anglos and Mexican authorities were established. Nevertheless, the majority of colonists from the United States were willing to remain within the Mexican union, provided that they had control of Texas as a separate state. Revolution was not an immediate threat when Houston arrived.

Houston rode southward from the Red River to Nacogdoches and then southwestward to San Felipe de Austin. Stephen F. Austin was not at home, but there Houston found an old acquaintance, the fabled Jim Bowie, who traveled with him to San Antonio. Bowie had come to Texas in 1828, married Ursula María de Veramendi, daughter of the vice-governor of Coahuila and Texas, and acquired huge landholdings in the state. He had been in Nacogdoches earlier in 1832, when Colonel José de las Piedras surrendered to Anglo settlers, and no doubt told Houston of the disturbances. After reaching San Antonio, Houston met with chiefs of the Comanches and secured their promise to attend a meeting with United States commissioners and the southeastern Indians at Fort Gibson in the spring of 1833.

With his mission to the Indians completed, Houston returned to San Felipe and applied as a married man for a league of land on Karankawa Bayou in Galveston County. He and Austin quickly reached an agreement that gave him a 4,428-acre stake in the future of Texas. Houston then headed for Nacogdoches, where he agreed to be a candidate for election to the convention scheduled to meet in April, and then traveled on to Natchitoches, Louisiana. There he wrote to the Indian commissioners at Fort Gibson describing his contacts with the Comanches and noting his intention of meeting the chiefs again near San Antonio prior to their trip to the fort for treaty negotiations. He also sent a letter to Andrew Jackson giving his first enthusiastic impressions of Texas, which he pronounced "the finest country to its extent upon the Globe." He had no doubt that "the country East of the River Grand of the North, would sustain a population of ten millions of souls." The Texas convention in April, he continued, would "declare all that country as Texas proper, and form a State Constitution." He expected to make Texas his "abiding place" but would *"never forget* the Country" of his birth.

Houston also expressed the opinion that Texas was governed very poorly and that unless the province attained separate statehood there would be a move to break away entirely from Mexico. In that event, he continued, the Mexicans, unable to control Texas and needing money, would transfer the province to some other power—if not the United States, then Great Britain, which wanted Texas badly. Houston probably exaggerated the degree of revolutionary sentiment in the province at that moment, but in pointing to the conflicting interests of the United States and Britain he put his finger on an issue critical to Texas's future. Most leaders in Washington hated the thought of British control in Texas, and Texans, particularly Houston, would eventually take advantage of that fear in their efforts to become part of the United States.

Determined to cast his lot with Texas, Houston returned to Nacogdoches by March 1, 1833, and although still a resident in intention only, won election to the convention that met in San Felipe on April 1. At this meeting, he helped William H. Wharton, a leader of the so-called war party that wanted to take a strong stand against Mexico, defeat Stephen F. Austin for the position of chairman, supported the call for separate statehood, and served on the committee that wrote a proposed constitution for the Mexican state of Texas. Not surprisingly, this constitution drew heavily on the fundamental laws of Tennessee and Louisiana. It prohibited banks and banking, a step that suited Houston's Jacksonian biases, but that he insisted was "politic" because Mexico had similar constitutional prohibitions on banking.

Once the convention completed its work and had to choose someone to present the petition for statehood and the proposed constitution in Mexico City, Houston insisted on being practical, on taking a sensible approach best calculated to bring success. Stephen F. Austin was well known and respected by Mexican officials and therefore logically the leader to take the convention's work to the capital city. However, Austin did not believe that a petition and constitution should be submitted without prior approval from the Mexican government, and consequently the "war party" tried to exclude him from the mission just as they had from the chairmanship of the convention. Houston, although originally a "war party" man, supported Austin in the belief that separate statehood could not be won without his involvement. The empresario, out of his sense of duty and love of Texas, accepted the thankless task of presenting a petition that was not of his creation to a government likely to think of it as an act of rebellion.

Houston had intended to return to San Antonio in late April or early May and accompany the Comanche chiefs on their projected visit to meet U.S. commissioners at Fort Gibson, but he did not do so for fear that he would alarm Mexican officials. The Mexicans, he later informed Secretary of War Lewis Cass, are always at war with the Comanches, and would suspect some "covert design" if the United States negotiated with the Indians. Houston did go to Fort Gibson for the projected meeting in late May, but neither the U.S. commissioners nor the Comanches appeared. His mission to the Indians having come to nothing, and his old shoulder wound aggravated by traveling, he then spent most of the summer resting at Hot Springs, Arkansas.

Back in Nacogdoches in the fall of 1833, Houston established a law practice, aided undoubtedly by the presence of several influential friends. Adolphus Sterne, a German-born Jew who had migrated to New Orleans and then on to Texas, was a leading merchant and public official in Nacogdoches. He and his wife, Eva, invited Houston to board in their home, a much more pleasant place to live than the local tavern. Henry Raguet, a native of Pennsylvania and a recent arrival like Houston, had prospered rapidly as a storekeeper. Raguet's oldest daughter, 17-year-old Anna, soon brought out Houston's weakness for young, beautiful women. She was well educated, especially in languages, and he asked her to teach him Spanish. He made only modest progress with the language and, likewise, with Anna, over whom he developed a friendly rivalry with a local doctor, Robert A. Irion, that continued for years.

In November 1833, Houston had Jonas Harrison, another Nacogdoches lawyer, petition local authorities for a divorce from

Eliza Allen, citing as justifications the length of his separation from her and the impossibility of reconciliation. Why he chose to act at that time is not clear. Perhaps it was another way of showing that Texas was a land of new beginnings. Indeed, the petition contained some interesting arguments about how Texas, "untrammeled and unbound by the fetters of precedent," could be liberal in the granting of divorces. In any case, no action took place on the petition until 1837, and Houston remained officially married. Houston joined the Catholic Church only a few weeks after filing for divorce. Church membership was a requirement for owning land and practicing law, so he, like most Anglos in Texas, simply acted from necessity.

Houston embarked on a lengthy trip to the East in 1834. He spent several months in Washington, where he visited President Jackson and successfully appealed for remission of his fine in the Stanbery affair, and paid short visits to New York, where he renewed contact with James Prentiss. He agreed to represent Prentiss as an individual seeking land grants in Texas but remained uninvolved in the Galveston Bay and Texas Land Company. In response to inquiries from Prentiss as to conditions in Texas, Houston on April 20, 1834, offered the following "candid impressions": "I do not think that it will be acquired by the U[nited] States. I do think that within one year it will be a Sovereign State [within the Mexican federal union] and acting in all things as such. Within three years I think it will be separated from the Mexican Confederacy, and remain so forever.... I assure you Santa Anna aspires to the *Purple*, and should he assume it, you know Texas is off from them, and so to remain." He concluded by remarking that these possibilities were "not pleasant to me" and that Prentiss should file them to see "how well I *prophesy*." As Houston headed back for Texas in late 1834, rumors of his intention to lead a revolution continued to circulate, but he was simply keeping an eye on developments and hoping for the best. As he wrote Prentiss on April 24, the course that he would pursue toward Texas was intended "if it can be done, as it ought to be; to preserve her integrity to the Confederacy of Mexico."

During the winter and spring of 1835, Houston practiced law in Nacogdoches and San Augustine and continued his courtship of Anna Raguet. He made another lasting friendship when Thomas Jefferson Rusk arrived from Georgia in pursuit of men who had swindled him in a mining venture and found that, although he could not recover his money, he liked the area enough to bring his family and remain there. Houston was one of the witnesses in February 1835, when Rusk took his oath of loyalty to Mexico. In May, Don Samuel Pablo Houston, as he was now formally titled, received another league of land, this one in the colony sponsored by David G. Burnet in East Texas. Observers said that he still drank too heavily, but his life was more settled than it had been at any time since his failed marriage.

Developments in Mexico during those years, however, soon proved profoundly unsettling. When Stephen F. Austin reached Mexico City in July 1833 on his mission to present the second San Felipe convention's petition for separate statehood for Texas, he found the central government, as usual, unstable and confusing. General Santa Anna, the hero of the revolt against Bustamante in 1832, had been elected president, with Valentín Gómez Farías as his vice president. Following their inauguration in April 1833, Santa Anna left the work of governing largely in the hands of Gómez Farías, apparently with the intention of allowing the vice president to lead a reform movement and then judging the reaction before taking power himself. Under these circumstances, Texas benefited from several significant reforms in 1833 to 1834, including religious toleration, the acceptance of English as a legal language, trial by jury, increased representation in the state legislature, and repeal of the part of the Law of April 6, 1830, that prohibited immigration from the United States. Anglos in Texas apparently responded favorably to these changes; at least that was the conclusion of Colonel Juan N. Almonte, who toured the province for Vice President Gómez Farías in 1834. Almonte, who had been educated in the United States and spoke English fluently, reported that the population of more than 20,000 enjoyed general prosperity and exhibited no discontent with their political condition.

Anglo-Texans probably were pleased with the reforms, but they had an additional reason in 1834 for keeping quiet. Austin had run into personal difficulties in Mexico, and it appeared that trouble in Texas might endanger his life. The empresario's problems arose because Gómez Farías, although supporting numerous reforms, would not approve separate statehood for Texas. Austin then told the vice president that the province was virtually separated from Coahuila anyhow, and in October 1833, he wrote a letter to elected local officials at San Antonio urging them to go ahead and plan to implement state government. Apparently because of this letter, he was arrested in January 1834, as he headed home from Mexico City, and held without charges or trial for a year and a half. In this situation, Austin's friends—including Houston, who had promised to support the empresario for any position that he might want in a separate state government—thought it necessary to be very careful in dealing with Mexico.

While Austin remained in confinement, Santa Anna proved correct Houston's prediction that the Mexican president aspired "to the purple." Seeing that Gómez Farías's liberal federalism had drawn the wrath of the church and the military in Mexico, Santa Anna became a conservative centralist as the means to taking absolute power. He resumed control of the presidency in May 1834 and within a year had the Mexican Congress abolish all constitutional restrictions on the central government and his office, which in effect made him a virtual dictator. Santa Anna, the Napoleon of the West, as he fancied himself, suppressed with great brutality the resistance that appeared in some states. After defeating the rebels in Zacatecas in May 1835, for example, he unleashed his troops on the city for two days of pillage that cost the lives of more than 2,000 defenseless inhabitants. In October 1835, Santa Anna completed the process of centralizing Mexico by abolishing all state legislatures and replacing them with military districts run by commanders appointed by the president.

Anglo-Texans reacted slowly to these developments, in part because of Austin's situation, but also because they had long viewed Santa Anna as a federalist. Moreover, the government of Coahuila and Texas had recently engaged in notoriously corrupt land deals so that some Texans thought that state governments deserved to be destroyed. By midsummer 1835, however, the real meaning of Santa Anna's move to centralism became clear, and trouble began. Conflict came first over customs collection at

Anahuac. In January 1835, Santa Anna had sent a collector to Anahuac with a 40-man detachment to restore the fort there. A dispute developed over the payment of duties, which Anglos at Anahuac complained were higher than those paid at Velasco and the new seaport town of Galveston, and Texans threatened to attack the Mexican fort. When news of this dispute reached General Martín Perfecto de Cós—Santa Anna's brother-in-law and commander of all northeastern Mexico—he sent a dispatch to Anahuac promising reinforcements. The courier stopped at San Felipe, however, whereupon Texan hotheads opened the letter and reacted by sending William Barrett Travis in command of a group of armed men to demand surrender of the fort. Travis accomplished his mission on June 30, 1835.

Much to the disgust of "war party" men such as Travis, the reaction among Anglos across Texas was strongly negative. The majority still wanted no action that might put their province in open opposition to the central government, and many appealed directly to General Cós, protesting their loyalty to Mexico. Cós, however, did not believe the Texans. Angry at their disrespect for Mexican authority, and his suspicions fanned by reports of Anglo disloyalty from the commander at San Antonio, the general demanded that Texans prove their loyalty by turning over for trial a number of radicals and troublemakers, including Travis, Robert M. Williamson, Frank W. Johnson, and Lorenzo de Zavala, a liberal from Yucatán who had fled to Texas to escape Santa Anna. Anglos refused to turn over anyone for trial by military tribunal, and Cós reacted by preparing to send a large army into Texas. By August 1835, a conflict with revolutionary possibilities was at hand.

Sam Houston, living quietly in Nacogdoches, had no immediate knowledge of these developments. In August 1835, Moseley Baker, a "war party" man from San Felipe, visited him in Nacogdoches with news of the threat from General Cós, but Houston, influenced by the still-strong sentiment for peace in East Texas as well as his own predilection for caution, urged Baker to calm down. His views began to change after Austin, finally released from confinement in Mexico City, arrived home in early September and expressed the view that war was necessary. "We must defend our rights ourselves," Austin said, "and our country by force of arms." Houston chaired a meeting in Nacogdoches on September 14 that discussed calling a consultation of representatives from across Texas, an idea that was quickly gaining popular support. On October 5, he gave Isaac Parker a letter to use in promoting Texas's cause in the United States, saying that war was inevitable and urging volunteers to aid their Anglo brethren. "Let each man come with a good rifle," he wrote, "and one hundred rounds of ammunition, and to come soon." Even then, however, Houston was careful not to get ahead of events or opinion. "Our principles are to support the constitution," he said, "and *down with the Usurper*!!!"

Houston's caution did not discourage support for him in Nacogdoches. On October 6, the local committee of safety appointed him commander in chief of armed forces in the Department of Nacogdoches, and two days later he directed the formation of 50-man companies that would elect their officers and report to him for orders. "The work of liberty has begun," he told his soldiers, but he was also careful to point out that the fight was against dictatorship and for the Mexican Constitution. Once more he called for volunteers, promising "liberal bounties of land" as a reward.

Even before Houston began military preparations in East Texas, fighting had begun at Gonzales. Mexican troops from San Antonio, under orders to recover a small cannon given earlier to settlers at Gonzales for defense against Indians, were fired upon on October 2 by Texans under the famed "Come and Take It" banner. One week later, General Cós reached San Antonio with an army of 300 men. He had come by sea from Matamoros, landed at Copano Bay, and reinforced the fort at Goliad on his way to San Antonio, but Texans closed in behind him and took Goliad on October 9. At that point, San Antonio was the only position in Texas under Mexican control. Soon, an army under the command of Stephen F. Austin moved to beseige it.

Houston, working on military preparations in East Texas, was not involved in the first fighting of the revolution; instead, he moved toward center stage by playing a major role in early political developments. The Consultation—called by several meetings and committees of safety during the late summer—assembled in Columbia on October 16–17, 1835, but having no quorum, postponed action until November 1. Houston, elected a delegate from Nacogdoches, arrived in late October and, learning that many of the others were with Austin's army near San Antonio, rode on in an effort to bring back enough delegates to create a quorum. Austin, who was not a man of military temperament, was discouraged from trying to deal with an army of undisciplined and ill-equipped volunteers, but he agreed that delegates to the Consultation should immediately go to San Felipe. This decision, approved by the army, allowed the Consultation to assemble with a quorum on November 1, 1835, although all the delegates were from eastern and central Texas.

At the Consultation, Houston attempted "to harmonize the feelings of the people and to produce unanimity of sentiment." He completed his break with the "war party" by successfully opposing an immediate declaration of independence in favor of a statement explaining the taking up of arms as a fight for statehood under the Constitution of 1824.

The Consultation set up a provisional government for the State of Texas, consisting of a governor, lieutenant governor, and a representative legislative body called the General Council. Henry Smith, a hot-tempered "war party" man from Brazoria, defeated Stephen F. Austin for the governor's office, and James W. Robinson, a "peace party" man from Nacogdoches, won the lieutenant governorship. Then, on November 12, Sam Houston was chosen commander in chief of all the Texas armies. Although the vote was overwhelming, the election became controversial. Moseley Baker contended that the men at San Antonio could hardly believe the choice, probably because other potential candidates such as Jim Bowie, Edward Burleson, and James W. Fannin were actually with the army. Moreover, Austin had written to the Consultation recommending a search for a trained military man to serve as general. In any case, Sam Houston had command. Texas's vast expanses of open land had attracted thousands of Anglo settlers. Their future now depended on success on the battlefield, and it was Houston's to win or lose.

CHAPTER FIVE

"If I Err, the Blame Is Mine"

❖
❖

Major General and Commander in Chief Sam Houston set up headquarters at the Virginia House in San Felipe on November 13, 1835, and began to develop a strategy for the probable war with Mexico. A letter of that date—inviting James W. Fannin to leave the volunteer army at San Antonio and join him as inspector general of the regular forces with the rank of colonel—indicated that his approach would be cautious and essentially defensive. Why not, he asked Fannin, fall back to Goliad and Gonzales, key positions for defending the interior, and leave Cós's army in San Antonio until Texan forces had artillery and sufficient strength to take the city? "Remember one Maxim," he wrote, "it is better to do well, *late*; than *never*! The army without means ought never to have passed the Guadalupe [Gonzales] without the proper munitions of war to reduce San Antonio. Therefore the error cannot be in falling back to an eligible position."

Fannin rejected Houston's offer, a response that foreshadowed the insurmountable difficulties the commander in chief would face during the next few months in creating and directing a regular army. Although ten years younger than Houston, Fannin had an exaggerated notion of his military ability. He thought that he should be appointed a brigadier general and made second in command. Houston could not have made such an appointment, even had he wished to, because all field officers were to be chosen by the governor and the General Council. And therein lay another problem—the council would not act. The commander in chief wrote to Smith and the council on December 5, pointing out that he could not discharge his duties until regular army officers were appointed and rewards for volunteer soldiers established. He was about to discover that with his expansive title went virtually no army or authority.

Ironically, a Texan success at San Antonio contributed heavily to destroying any chance Houston had of creating a unified army and adopting a defensive strategy. Stephen F. Austin, charged by the Consultation with leading a mission to seek aid for Texas in the United States, had given up command of the volunteer forces besieging General Cós on November 24, and Edward Burleson had been elected to succeed him. By early December, his army hungry and not clothed for cold weather, Burleson considered retreating to Goliad for the winter, but a Mexican deserter told him that the town was poorly defended. Benjamin Milam, a Kentuckian who had spent years adventuring in the borderlands, called out: "Who will go with old Ben Milam into San Antonio?" More than 500 volunteers came forward, and the attack began on the morning of December 5. After five days of fighting from house to house, during which Milam was killed, General Cós surrendered. The victorious Texans permitted Cós and his soldiers to return to Mexico south of the Rio Grande, after promising to support the Constitution of 1824.

The taking of San Antonio, which cost the Texan forces only 12 dead and 18 wounded, created unreasonable optimism among the victors. A few hundred men, many of them volunteers from the United States, remained at the Alamo, the old Spanish mission that had been converted into a fort, under the command of Colonel James C. Neill, and most of the soldiers from Texas went home. Many believed that, with no Mexican soldiers left in Texas, the war was over. Houston differed, indicating in a proclamation issued on December 12 that, regardless of the outcome at San Antonio, Texas needed a trained army of 5,000 men by March 1, 1836. He was correct, for Santa Anna had already begun to prepare a force to cross the Rio Grande, but within the government at San Felipe, chaos reigned. The General Council finally appointed a few field officers but did nothing else to organize, discipline, and train an army during the winter of 1836.

Rather than supporting the commander in chief in readying for the inevitable invasion, the General Council increasingly acted under the influence of what Houston later called "busy, noisy, second-rate men" who always wanted "rash and extreme measures." When Dr. James Grant and Francis W. Johnson—two of the leaders in the victory at San Antonio—argued that an expedition to attack Matamoros would bring rich spoils of war, attract the support of Mexican liberals, and be the best means of defense for Texas, the General Council listened receptively. Houston immediately disagreed, as did Governor Smith, but in mid-December the Council, coming increasingly under the control of men who wished to take over direction of all military operations, ordered the commander in chief to shift his headquarters to Washington-on-the-Brazos, a tiny settlement 40 miles north of San Felipe. Although Houston knew that he was being put out of the way, he, as always, bowed to civil authority. He did permit himself a letter to Governor Smith, pointing out "the difficulties which are thrown in the way of all my exertions to promote the cause of the country." The holiday season at his new headquarters left him "most miserably cool & sober—so you can [say] to all my friends," he wrote. "Instead of Egg-nog, I eat roasted eggs in my office."

In early January 1836, Houston learned that the General Council had authorized the Matamoros expedition and permitted Johnson and Grant to strip the Alamo of all but about eighty soldiers. Both Johnson and James W. Fannin had been given command without any indication as to which was superior. Houston saw these developments as a recipe for disaster and begged Governor Smith to call the council into session and "adopt some course that will redeem our country from a state of deplorable anarchy." He concluded: "No language can express the anguish of my soul.... What will the world think of the authorities of Texas?"

Houston decided that the only way to deal with the proposed Matamoros expedition was to go to the army, so he left Washington-on-the-Brazos for Goliad on January 8, 1836. Reaching that point late on the fourteenth, he found neither Fannin, Johnson, nor Grant present. Fannin was recruiting volunteers for the expedition, promising to pay them with spoils taken from the enemy. Johnson was probably at San Felipe talking to the General Council; and Grant, at Refugio, another 25 miles to the southwest. The next morning Houston addressed the soldiers gathered at Goliad, pleading with them to withdraw from the proposed expedition against Matamoros. To attack into Mexico while expecting spoils as pay, he warned, would be piracy rather than war. Moreover, he told the soldiers, other Mexican states would not join the cause, so Texas should declare independence and then defend it at home.

Before Houston finished speaking a courier arrived from San Antonio with a report that two of Santa Anna's generals had crossed the Rio Grande. Colonel Neill commanding at the Alamo wanted help. Shortly thereafter, Jim Bowie reached Goliad with the intention of leading volunteers back to San Antonio. About thirty men joined him, and as he left on January 17, Houston sent orders to Colonel Neill to remove the cannon and ammunition, demolish the Alamo, and retreat to Gonzales. But then, perhaps swayed by Bowie's belief that the fortress could not be taken, he gave Neill, who was on the spot, discretion to make the final decision himself. Houston informed Governor Smith of these developments, saying that he would go to San Antonio himself were the "Matamoros rage" not so great. Believing the planned expedition even more foolish in light of the reported Mexican invasion, he intended to go on to Refugio, make contact with volunteer units that were likely to join Fannin, and await orders from the governor. Clearly he hoped to receive support in stopping the expedition.

When Houston reached Refugio, he again found none of the would-be commanding officers present, but on the twentieth, Johnson arrived with orders from the General Council that gave Fannin and himself control of the volunteers who would attack Matamoros. Houston still supposedly commanded the regular army, but no such force existed. Johnson also told Houston that Governor Smith had attacked the council for acting without his approval and had in response been deposed in favor of Lieutenant Governor Robinson. Any semblance of orderly government had disappeared, and the commander in chief's enemies had control of what remained. Under these circumstances, Houston decided that he would return to Washington-on-the-Brazos and report to Smith, who had refused to accept the council's removal order. To remain with the Matamoros expedition would be to open himself to the blame that would follow its almost certain failure. Before leaving Refugio, Houston addressed the soldiers assembled there, telling them about the council's actions and explaining that if they thought deposing the governor and taking away the commander in chief's authority over volunteers were illegal acts, they were not obligated to move toward Matamoros. About two hundred men decided not to go, leaving between sixty and seventy with Johnson. Houston's opposition reduced support for the expedition, which was foolish and unnecessary from the outset and probably would have come to nothing in any event. At least his actions reduced the number of men who became easy prey for Mexican cavalry in south Texas during the spring of 1836.

Houston left Refugio during the night of January 20 and rode toward San Felipe to report to Governor Smith. Silent and gloomy for much of the trip, he contemplated simply quitting and burying himself in what he later called "the solitude of nature." On this occasion, however, there would be no voluntary exile. Texas had become the purpose of Houston's life, and "the world could not move him" from it. On January 30, he sent Governor Smith a long summary of the month's events. "The evil is now done," he wrote in reference to the Matamoros expedition and the actions of the General Council, but "I trust sincerely, that the first of March may establish a government on some permanent foundation, where honest functionaries will regard and execute the known and established laws of the country, agreeable to their oaths." Fortunately, back in December 1835, the General Council had called a new convention to meet at Washington-on-the-Brazos on March 1, 1836. Houston now rested his hopes for Texas's future on that meeting and asked for a furlough from his duties until it met.

Houston went to Nacogdoches in early February 1836. He visited the Raguet family where, according to legend, 20-year-old Anna promised to make a silk sash for his uniform. Nacogdoches voters refused to make him a delegate to the convention, but, fortunately, he won a seat representing Refugio, a settlement that he had visited only once. Houston then spent the rest of February on a mission to the Cherokee Indians of northeast Texas. Alarmed by reports that the Cherokees might join the Mexicans, the Consultation had promised to support the Indians' rights to land granted them by Mexico, and on December 28, 1835, Governor Smith had appointed Houston and two others to negotiate a treaty assuring their neutrality. At the village of Chief Duwali (usually called the Bowl or Bowles by Anglos), leader of the Texas Cherokees, Houston signed a treaty that declared "a firm and lasting peace forever" and guaranteed the Indians' claims to lands in northeast Texas. More than likely Houston told Duwali that the treaty had to be ratified, but he had no idea how difficult that would prove. He gave the chief a sword during ceremonies after the signing and returned to Nacogdoches, convinced that the Indians had been treated fairly. Stopping at Raguet's once more, he found that Anna had completed his silk sash. She tied it around his waist, and he headed for Washington-on-the-Brazos.

Houston's arrival at the convention site on February 27 created, in the words of one observer, "more sensation than that of any other man. He is evidently the people's man, and seems to take pains to ingratiate himself with everybody." Later that same day a courier from San Antonio brought the terrifying news that General Santa Anna with an army in the thousands had invaded Texas and besieged the Alamo with its 150 defenders. Although he had never considered San Antonio critical to the defense of Texas, Houston's evacuation order taken to Colonel Neill by Jim Bowie in January had left room for independent judgment. Neill, who became ill and left the Alamo on February 11, Bowie, and William B. Travis—who arrived at the Alamo under orders from Governor Smith in early February and took over sole command on the twenty-fourth when Bowie fell ill—all believed that defense of the Alamo was essential in order to deny the Mexicans the primary road into the interior of Texas. Houston probably still disagreed, but the arrival of Santa Anna pushed aside all issues of judgment to that point. The question for the men at Washington-on-the-Brazos was what to do next. Some wanted to march to San Antonio, but Houston's advice was that they attend to the business at hand, the setting up of an effective government.

Fifty-nine men assembled on March 1, and the next day, Sam Houston's forty-third birthday, adopted a declaration of independence. Acting under his old commission as commander in chief, Houston immediately issued a proclamation appealing to all Texans to come to the aid of those besieged at San Antonio. "*Independence is declared,*" he said, "it must be maintained." Two days later, the convention, with only one negative vote, passed a resolution making Sam Houston "commander in chief of the land forces of the Texian Army both Regulars, Volunteers, and Militia while in actual service." His speech of acceptance expressed the belief that this commission was both specific and encompassing enough to prevent the problems he had encountered with the General Council. Houston did not immediately leave the convention and may have intended to participate in the remaining work of writing a constitution and creating an interim government for the Republic of Texas, but then on Sunday morning, March 6, another message arrived from the Alamo. Santa Anna has raised "a blood-red banner," meaning "vengeance against rebels," Travis wrote, and demanded surrender without terms concerning the lives of prisoners. When Richard Ellis, president of the convention, finished reading this message, Robert Potter from Nacogdoches proposed that the delegates march to the relief of the Alamo. Houston quickly responded with an hour-long speech urging the convention to remain calm and complete its work. He promised to leave immediately for Gonzales and lead the small force of Texans gathering there in defending the convention and, if possible, relieving the Alamo. Without waiting for a vote, he left the hall. The convention remained in session until March 17, wrote a constitution, and set up an interim government with David G. Burnet as president and Lorenzo de Zavala as vice president to lead the Republic until regular elections could be held.

Houston left for the 150-mile ride to Gonzales accompanied by George Hockley and two others. He was again a commander in chief with in effect no army, the only Texan forces in the field being the men trapped in the Alamo, a group of about 400 gathered by Fannin at Goliad as part of the Matamoros expedition, and the volunteers assembling at Gonzales. He did not know it, but the men who had ignored his advice in January and stayed with Johnson and Grant had already fallen prey to Mexican cavalry commanded by Colonel José Urrea. Santa Anna's most efficient officer, Urrea had crossed the Rio Grande at Matamoros with 1,500 men and moved along the Gulf coast, catching Johnson at San Patricio on February 27 and Grant at Agua Dulce Creek on March 2, killing or capturing more than sixty Texans. Only Johnson and four others escaped.

Houston's little party rode hard on the sixth and reached open prairie by night. The next morning, he listened in vain for the signal gun that Travis had promised to fire each day to indicate that the Alamo had not fallen, and then, fearing the worst, wrote to the convention urging the delegates to declare that Texas had been part of the United States since the Louisiana Purchase. This suggests a belief that Texas might be overmatched against Mexico and therefore had to have help from the United States.

On March 9, still maintaining some hope of relieving the Alamo, Houston sent orders to Fannin to abandon Goliad and meet him on Cibolo Creek between San Antonio and Gonzales. He would not have been heartened had he known that Fannin had once before, in response to a plea from Travis, attempted to move his troops and then given in to delay and indecision and done nothing. When he reached Gonzales on March 11 after a trip hampered by bad weather and high rivers, Houston found 374 volunteers under the command of Edward Burleson. He began to organize this force into a regiment but was interrupted by the arrival of two Mexicans with the news that Santa Anna's army had taken the Alamo on the sixth, killed all the defenders including those who attempted to surrender, and burned their bodies. This "cold blooded massacre," he wrote later, "stirred up a feeling that was never to sleep again." No longer needing Fannin to help at San Antonio, Houston ordered him to retreat to Victoria, on the east side of the Guadalupe River, and take up a defensive position that would enable the two remaining Texan armies to support each other. The commander in chief's orders were sound, but, as usual, Fannin did not obey.

On March 13, wanting to be certain that he had heard the truth about the fall of the Alamo, Houston sent Henry Karnes and Erastus "Deaf" Smith to San Antonio. They returned early that night, bringing Susannah Dickenson, the widow of one of the defenders, her child, and two black servants with the news that the Alamo had fallen as reported and that Santa Anna's army, estimated at as many as 5,000 men, was advancing on Gonzales. In fact, although Houston had no idea of it, the Mexican commander had devised a three-pronged movement across Texas—an army commanded by General Antonio Gaona was to swing north from San Antonio and proceed to Nacogdoches by the upper crossing of the Trinity; Colonel Urrea's cavalry was to advance along the coast from Matamoros toward Galveston; and the main force under General Vicente Filisola was to move directly into the heart of the province. Santa Anna himself intended to stay with the main army only until about April 1, when he was to be picked up by ship at Matagorda. He expected no more resistance, but planned nevertheless, as Houston wrote later, to unleash "three rolling streams of fire" to "cover the land with devastation." Santa Anna meant to teach the Texans the lesson that he had taught the people of Zacatecas.

Faced by overwhelming numbers and fearing that Fannin had been caught before he could leave Goliad, Houston saw no choice but to retreat. "By falling back," he explained to James Collinsworth, chairman of the military committee at the convention, "Texas can rally, and defeat any force that can come against her." His army of fewer than 400 men left Gonzales before midnight on the thirteenth and headed eastward toward Burnham's Crossing on the Colorado River near present-day LaGrange. The rear guard, without Houston's orders, burned the town as they departed. By the time his force—worn out from marching through rain and mud—reached the Colorado on the afternoon of the seventeenth, volunteers arriving from the east had increased its number to about 600. However, word of the massacre at the Alamo frightened off some would-be soldiers and created panic among the civilian population. Taking no time for preparation, settlers loaded what belongings they could onto any means of conveyance and headed east. Fearful of Mexicans and Indians and made even more miserable by the weather, throwing away possessions as they went, the refugees clogged the roads and fought for places on ferries at rain-swollen rivers. Texans would call this flight the "Runaway Scrape." It made Houston's task all the more difficult.

At the Colorado, Houston had the army assist all the refugees in crossing the river, then moved his men to the east side also and held them there for two days, in part as a shield for the civilians who moved on toward San Felipe on the Brazos and in part because he held some hope of being able to make a stand at that point. Fifteen hundred Texans can "defeat all that Santa Anna can send to the Colorado," he informed Collinsworth on the seventeenth, and asked that all available men be rushed to that point. On the morning of March 19, after two days at Burnham's, Houston moved his army about 25 miles down the Colorado to Beason's Ferry at present-day Columbus. He still hoped to fight at the river, but if further retreat became necessary, his force could use the Cushatti Trace, a better road on high ground, to reach San Felipe. As usual, Houston sought to keep open as many options as possible.

On March 22, two days after the army reached Beason's Ferry, scouts reported that an advance unit of the Mexican army commanded by General Joaquín Ramírez y Sesma had reached the west bank of the Colorado three miles above the Texans' position on the east side. Having 600 cavalry and 150 infantry under his command and only two artillery pieces, Ramírez y Sesma seemingly gave Houston what he had hoped for—an opportunity to attack a Mexican force of approximately equal size. The next day, however, brought several pieces of news that caused the Texan commander to hesitate. First, he learned that leaders of the provisional government had become frightened at rumors of the Mexican advance and fled from Washington-on-the-Brazos to Harrisburg on Buffalo Bayou. "The retreat of the government will have a bad effect on the troops," Houston wrote interim secretary of war Thomas J. Rusk, "and I am half-provoked at it myself." Second, a report arrived that Fannin had begun his move toward Victoria on March 19, five days after receiving the order to retreat, but had been surrounded by Urrea's cavalry on an open prairie near Coleto Creek. The outcome of the battle was not yet known, but Houston expected the worst.

Two days later word came that Fannin had been forced to surrender on the twentieth and that Urrea's cavalry was pushing on toward the Colorado. At the same time, Smith and Karnes brought in several prisoners and a message from Ramírez y Sesma addressed to General Santa Anna in San Antonio. Houston learned that the force facing his army across the Colorado had been reinforced, although he was unsure of the numbers involved, and he began to understand something of Santa Anna's strategy. With Urrea ready to cross the Colorado 40 miles south of Beason's Ferry and Gaona preparing to do the same at Bastrop 60 miles to the north, Houston decided that to risk the one remaining Texas army on an attack across the rain-swollen river would be foolish. Even if he won, he would have wounded men to care for and would be easily enveloped by the remaining Mexican armies. The only prudent course was to retreat to San Felipe on the Brazos.

Having sent scouting parties along the river to make the Mexicans believe that he was planning an attack, Houston moved his army eastward again after dark on March 26, leaving campfires burning to discourage pursuit. The army covered the 50 miles to San Felipe in less than three days, arriving there on the twenty-eighth. Many in the ranks complained that they wanted to fight rather than run and after reaching the Brazos were free with advice for Houston. Two captains, Moseley Baker and Wylie Martin, were particularly open in their criticism, promising the soldiers that another retreat would lead to a new commander in chief. "On my arrival on the Brazos," Houston wrote Rusk, "had I consulted the wishes of all, I should have been like the ass between two stacks of hay. Many wished me to go below [San Felipe], others above. I consulted none—I held no councils of war. If I err, the blame is mine." He decided to move northward about 20 miles along the west bank of the Brazos to the plantation of Jared Groce, one of the wealthiest men in Texas. A steamboat called the *Yellowstone* was at Groce's, offering the best means available for crossing the flooded river, and from that spot roads led to Nacogdoches and to Harrisburg, the location of the provisional government. Baker and Martin refused to move with the army to Groce's, so Houston ordered the former to remain and defend the crossing at San Felipe and the latter to go downriver and do the same at Fort Bend. This was not a militarily correct way to deal with insubordination, but under the circumstances it made sense.

Two days of suffering from "heavy rains and dreadful roads" brought the army on March 31 to Groce's, where Houston hoped to rest, receive supplies and additional men, and train his army. By that time, the fear sweeping Texas worried him nearly as much as did Santa Anna's armies. "For Heaven's sake," he wrote Rusk on the twenty-ninth, "do not drop back again with the seat of government! Your removal to Harrisburg has done more to increase the panic in the country than anything else that has occurred in Texas, except the fall of the Alamo." From Groce's on the thirty-first, he made the same plea. Do something, he urged, "to allay the fever and chill which prevails in the country, and let the people from the east march to the camp!" When promised reinforcements do not arrive, he told Rusk, the army's mood becomes worse.

The camp at Groce's offered some high ground suitable for drilling, so Houston remained there for ten days to prepare his army for battle. Gradually, although training was just as unpopular as retreat and some soldiers remained dissatisfied with their commander, the army's spirits improved. Then, on the night of April 3, word came concerning the fate of Fannin's men, and desire for revenge created new determination. After surrendering to Urrea on March 20, Fannin and his soldiers were held at Goliad. Several smaller groups of volunteers from the United States, who had been captured shortly after reaching Texas, were imprisoned there also, bringing the total to 430. On Palm Sunday, March 27, at Santa Anna's orders, Mexican officers marched the prisoners out of town in three columns and shot them. The wounded, including Fannin, were murdered in the fort. A few escaped and took word of the massacre east to the Brazos, where Houston, who had not wanted much talk about the Alamo, encouraged his army to discuss what had happened to Fannin. "The day of just retribution ought not to be deferred," he wrote Rusk.

Houston used the ten days at Groce's to drill his army, build its spirits, and increase its determination to fight, but David G. Burnet, interim president of the republic, had decided that the whole campaign was a disgrace. He wrote to the commander in chief demanding action. "The enemy are laughing you to scorn," he told Houston. "You must fight them. You must retreat no farther. The country expects you to fight. The salvation of the country depends on you doing so." Houston's reply was succinct and sarcastic. "I have kept the army together under most discouraging circumstances," he told Burnet, "and I hope a just and wise God, in whom I have always believed, will yet save Texas. . . . I am sorry that I am so wicked, for 'the prayers of the righteous shall prevail.' That you are so, I have no doubt, and hope that Heaven, as such, will help and prosper you, and crown your efforts with success in behalf of Texas and humanity." Differences between Houston and Burnet had appeared first at the convention; during the war the two became lifelong enemies.

On April 7, Houston received information that the Mexican army had reached San Felipe, and he issued an order telling his men that the time for battle was fast approaching. "The victims of the Alamo, and the names of those who were murdered at Goliad, call for *cool, deliberate* vengeance," he wrote. "Strict discipline, order, and subordination, will insure us the victory." Still, however, not knowing that Santa Anna had resumed command and was with the force at San Felipe or what the Mexicans would do next, he waited. Upon reaching the Brazos, Santa Anna learned that Houston was to the north at Groce's and the government to the southeast at Harrisburg. A Texan prisoner told him that Houston had only 800 men and would continue to retreat eastward across the Trinity, so the Mexican commander decided to pursue the government first and deal with the army later. Accordingly, he moved downriver to Fort Bend with the intention of crossing the Brazos there and moving directly toward Harrisburg.

When scouts reported on April 11 that the Mexicans were moving southward and probably intended to cross the Brazos, Houston saw that unless he crossed also, his army could be trapped between enemy forces on both sides of the river. He ordered all detachments defending crossings downriver to report to the main army at Donoho's farm on the road from Groce's to Harrisburg and, on the twelfth, had the *Yellowstone* begin ferrying his troops to the east bank. A pleasant surprise waited for him there—two 6-pound cannon donated by the citizens of Cincinnati. The "Twin Sisters," as the Texans dubbed these guns, did not exactly constitute an artillery unit, but they further inspired the army, which completed the river crossing on the fifteenth and marched the few miles to Donoho's farm before camping to await the arrival of detachments from downriver.

In the meantime, Houston received another letter from President Burnet, saying, "The country expects something from you." Sick of what he called "taunts and suggestions . . . gratuitously tendered to me," the commander in chief responded by reviewing the campaign to that point and indicating that he intended to fight when he had a chance of success. "I beg leave to assure you," he wrote, "that I will omit no opportunity to serve the country. . . ." Houston also sought to calm panic among the civilian population by issuing a proclamation expressing confidence that the Mexican army could be defeated east of the Brazos. "Come and free your country at once," he urged volunteers, "and be *men!*"

On April 16 Houston had his troops prepare to march southward on the road from Groce's to Harrisburg. Several recently arrived companies objected on the grounds that they needed time to rest and eat breakfast. Faced again with insubordination, Houston dealt with it, as before, by giving the dissidents something else to do. He ordered Captain Wylie Martin, the most persistent objector, to go east to the Trinity and look after refugees in that area. As that problem was being solved, a black, who said that he had been a prisoner of the Mexicans and had been released to act as a courier, rode up with a message that the Mexicans had crossed the Brazos and headed for Harrisburg. Houston was puzzled that a force of less than a thousand men with little artillery would set out in advance of the main army, but he did not hesitate to take advantage of an opportunity for a battle in which numbers would be relatively equal.

The Texas army, leaving behind a considerable number of men who had become sick with measles, covered 55 miles in two and a half days through what Houston called "the greatest possible difficulties." Heavy rain turned the road into a quagmire, and on numerous occasions men had to unload wagons, carry the contents across bogs, and then help the horses get the wagons through. Arriving at Buffalo Bayou opposite Harrisburg on April 18, Houston learned that the Mexican army had reached the town three days earlier but failed to catch the government there. President Burnet and the other officials had fled to New Washington on Galveston Bay. Santa Anna had decided to burn Harrisburg and continue in pursuit of the government, thinking that he could capture the leaders and then turn north, cross the San Jacinto River north of the bay, and intercept Houston's army trying to escape to the east. The Mexican force reached New Washington on the eighteenth, just as Houston came in behind them at Harrisburg, and once more narrowly failed to capture the government, which went by schooner down the bay to Galveston.

On April 19, Houston's scouts, Smith and Karnes, crossed Buffalo Bayou and returned with three Mexican couriers and a bonanza of vital information. The captive messengers, one of whom carried a pouch inscribed "W. B. Travis," had letters showing that Santa Anna personally was commanding the Mexican force then at New Washington and that, except for reinforcements being rushed forward under General Cós, all other enemy troops were west of the Brazos. Houston saw immediately the opportunity presented by these circumstances. He and Rusk, who had joined the army in early April, issued one more appeal for volunteers, and he prepared a formal letter to Rusk that amounted to an explanation and justification of the action he was about to take. "We will only be about seven hundred to march, besides the camp guard," he wrote. "*But we go to conquest.* It is wisdom growing out of necessity to meet and fight the enemy *now*. Every consideration enforces it." The cautious commander wanted everyone to know that he had not made a rash decision.

Leaving behind its baggage and another sizable group of men who had contracted measles, Houston's army crossed Buffalo Bayou on the nineteenth, using a ferryboat located two miles east of Harrisburg. Just before dark, the crossing completed, the commander in chief ordered his men into formation and told them that a fight with Santa Anna was at hand. He invited all those who wanted to avoid the battle to leave and, when no one moved, gave them a battle cry—"Remember the Alamo." "This watchword," he said later, "was caught up by every man in the army, and one simultaneous shout broke up into the sky...." The Texans then moved eastward during the night until they became so tired that Houston had to give them several hours of rest. Back on their feet at daylight, the soldiers continued the march until allowed to stop and prepare breakfast sometime after sunrise. Just then, scouts came in with the information that Santa Anna had burned New Washington and was heading for Lynch's Ferry on the San Jacinto River immediately to the south of the mouth of Buffalo Bayou. Anxious to reach the ferry before the Mexicans and pick his position, Houston ordered everything packed and rapidly marched his troops the remaining distance. The Texans made camp in the trees lining Buffalo Bayou and completed their breakfast. The boat that Santa Anna intended to use as a ferry on the San Jacinto was run up the bayou behind Houston's camp, and the "Twin Sisters" were placed in full view. To reach the ferry, which was to the Texans' left, the Mexicans would have to cross an open prairie in front of the guns and Houston's men sheltered in the timber.

About two o'clock in the afternoon of the twentieth, Santa Anna's army approached the San Jacinto and discovered the Texans. The Mexican force advanced to within 300 yards and opened fire with their 12-pounder cannon, but most of the shots crashed harmlessly overhead into the trees. When the infantry came forward as though to attack, the "Twin Sisters" fired grape-shot and cut-up horseshoes that, although aimed too high to inflict serious damage, discouraged any frontal attack. Santa Anna then withdrew to the south about three-quarters of a mile from the Texans' position and established a camp. Later in the day, Houston approved a request by Colonel Sidney Sherman that the cavalry reconnoiter the field but gave orders not to go within range of the Mexicans' guns or to provoke an attack. Sherman, however, drew fire from the Mexican infantry and became involved in a fight with enemy cavalry, all in Houston's opinion with the intention of bringing on a general fight between the two armies. One Texan was killed and two wounded, one of whom was rescued heroically by a recently arrived volunteer from Georgia named Mirabeau Bonaparte Lamar. Houston made Lamar a colonel and gave him command of the cavalry. The words that he had for Sherman earned him a lifetime of hatred.

On the night of April 20, while Santa Anna rested comfortably in his tent, Houston slept on the ground with no blanket, a coil of artillery rope serving as a pillow. April 21 dawned clear and bright, an omen, the commander thought, favoring battle. Around mid-morning General Cós arrived with about 550 reinforcements, bringing Santa Anna's total strength to nearly 1,350 men compared to fewer than 800 Texans. Houston refused to be discouraged, however, and told his soldiers that the troops they saw arriving had been there the day before and were simply being marched around to be seen again—a Mexican *ruse de guerre*. At noon he held a council of war with Rusk and the six field officers to discuss one question: Should the Texans attack or wait to be attacked? Five of the eight advised against attacking, but the commander in chief had made up his mind.

Santa Anna could receive further reinforcements only from the east along the road from Harrisburg to Lynch's Ferry, so immediately after the council of war, Houston gave axes to Deaf Smith and another volunteer and sent them to destroy the bridge over Vince's Bayou, a stream that crossed the road about 8 miles to the west of the probable battlefield. This step also cut off the only good route of retreat for either army. Then, at three o'clock in the afternoon, Houston ordered his 783 "effectives" into a battle formation that stretched across the prairie. Burleson's regiment occupied the center, with Sherman on the left and four companies of infantry under Lieutenant Colonel Henry Millard on the right. The "Twin Sisters" were placed in an advance position just to the right of Burleson, and Lamar's cavalry was positioned on the far right. At three-thirty the Texan line began to advance, the artillery hurriedly moving to within 200 yards of Santa Anna's camp while other units were ordered to hold their fire until reaching point-blank range. Cós's men, who were tired from marching through the night, had been allowed to eat and rest, and some of the officers, including Santa Anna, were enjoying an afternoon siesta, but Mexican pickets quickly detected the attack, and their artillery and infantry opened fire. The Texans had to cross a swale, or depression, in the prairie, however, so that fire from the 12-pounder went overhead, and infantry muskets were not effective at more than 100 yards. Once the "Twin Sisters" were in position, they began to blast the Mexicans' hastily constructed breastworks with grapeshot and pieces of horseshoes. Deaf Smith then galloped onto the field with the news that the bridge over Vince's Bayou was down, and all the while, the line of Texas infantry led by Houston on horseback advanced, crouching low in the tall grass, without firing.

The Mexicans waited until the Texans were within 60 yards before firing a concerted volley. As Houston put it, "the mass of their storm of lead went over the heads of the assailants," but he was not so fortunate. A musket ball shattered the front part of the tibia bone about an inch above his right ankle, and at least five struck his mount in the chest. The horse staggered but kept moving forward. Houston quickly led the infantry on to within 20 yards of the Mexican line, where the Texans delivered their one organized volley of the battle and then charged. Screaming "Remember the Alamo, Remember Goliad," they used their muskets as clubs and killed at close range with pistols and knives as well. Both wings of Santa Anna's line were rolled into the center, and 18 minutes after the beginning of close fighting, the Mexican camp was in Texan hands. At that point the battle became a slaughter as the Texas army practiced its own version of "no quarter" until twilight, killing hundreds of Mexican soldiers as they fled to the west toward the downed bridge over Vince's Bayou.

Houston attempted to stop the unnecessary slaughter and, where he could be present on the field, succeeded. Once the rout began, Colonel Juan N. Almonte and more than two hundred soldiers collected in a small grove of trees across a narrow bayou to the southeast of the original Mexican camp. Houston, after sending an officer to the west to enforce his order to stop the killing, rode toward Almonte's position. Reaching the bayou, he reined his horse sharply, and it fell dead. He jumped from the horse but could not stand on his wounded leg, so he gave command to Secretary of War Rusk to complete the battle. Almonte, however, surrendered, and organized Mexican resistance ended. Houston, remounted on a horse provided by one of his officers, rode across the field to his camp and lay down at the foot of an oak tree.

The victory at San Jacinto was, as Houston put it later, "almost a miracle." Texans killed 630 Mexican soldiers and captured 730 more, at a cost of 2 dead and 23 wounded, 6 of whom would later die. But, as Houston well knew, the battle left the army and its cause far from secure. Thousands of Mexican soldiers were a relatively short distance away on the Brazos, and the whereabouts of Santa Anna was unknown. Then, on the afternoon of April 22, a search party brought in a prisoner whom the other surviving Mexicans saluted and called El Presidente. The "Napoleon of the West" was at the mercy of Sam Houston. Some of the Texans wanted to execute Santa Anna immediately in retaliation for the Alamo and Goliad, but Houston knew that, alive, his prisoner was the key to removing all Mexican soldiers from Texas without further bloodshed. He refused Santa Anna's offer to negotiate a peace treaty, saying that was a matter for the government, and forced the Mexican commander to sign an armistice providing for an end to fighting and the removal of all Mexican armies south of the Rio Grande. Final peace negotiations were to be handled later by the governments of Mexico and Texas. Deaf Smith took the order to withdraw to General Filisola, who had assumed command upon the capture of Santa Anna and had already begun a retreat. The general promised to end hostilities and continued to move southwestward toward Mexico.

In spite of his wound, Houston remained at San Jacinto for two weeks after the battle, protecting Santa Anna and waiting for the government leaders to arrive. He also wrote an official report of the battle and a letter to Rusk arguing that the final peace settlement should guarantee independence to Texas with boundaries reaching to the Rio Grande and that Santa Anna should be held hostage until ratifications were exchanged. After a while, the stench from the dead—whom he could not persuade his soldiers to bury—forced him to move camp a mile and a half away. President Burnet and some of the cabinet finally arrived on May 4 and, apparently out of jealousy at Houston's success, immediately began to treat the commander in chief as a thief rather than a hero. They were especially upset that he had distributed the contents of Santa Anna's money chest to the soldiers, and Secretary of the Navy Robert Potter, who had opposed his election back in March, proposed dismissing him as commander in chief for that offense. Also, Houston was not allowed to attend the cabinet meeting that discussed what to do with Santa Anna.

By May 5, Houston's wound had become so inflamed and painful that his surgeon insisted on his going to New Orleans for treatment. He wrote a warm farewell to the army, placed temporarily under the command of Rusk, and prepared to leave for Galveston with the government leaders and Santa Anna on the *Yellowstone*. At that point, according to Houston, Burnet refused him passage, saying that his place was with the army. However, the captain of the *Yellowstone* would not leave without Houston, so he was allowed on board. When Surgeon General Alexander Ewing insisted on accompanying his patient, the new secretary of war, Mirabeau B. Lamar, dismissed him from the service for leaving his post. Departing on May 8, the steamboat reached Galveston by the eleventh, and Houston sought passage to New Orleans on the *Liberty*, a schooner belonging to the government of Texas. He was refused—apparently because Burnet wanted the commander in chief to leave without permission—and therefore had to sail on an American trading ship called the *Flora*. It looked as though the government wanted to exile him from Texas.

Sam Houston's San Jacinto campaign was not a headlong flight toward security in the United States but rather a strategic withdrawal away from a numerically superior enemy while building strength and waiting for an opportunity to strike an effective blow. The men who wanted to fight before April 21—if they could have had their way—would have, as Houston put it later, "cost another Alamo or Goliad tragedy, and the day of San Jacinto would never have come." In any case, Houston won, and Texas became independent. San Jacinto became his password to Texas heroism forever.

CHAPTER SIX

"Perfectly Aware of the Difficulties That Surround Me"

❖
❖

The *Flora* reached New Orleans on May 22, and a large crowd watched as the hero of the fight for Texas independence, haggard and weak from the leg wound that was wrapped only in a blood-stained shirt, managed to move unassisted from the boat to the dock before passing out on the litter provided to take him to the home of his friend, William Christy. Doctors drained the wound and removed numerous bone splinters, and Houston recovered rapidly. By June 1, he could sit up, although he declined an offer by the citizens of New Orleans of a public dinner in his honor, citing his health and a belief that he would be lacking in "respect for my adopted country . . . if I were to unite in any festive entertainments whilst Texas contains one individual hostile to her liberty." Houston's exploits had made him famous in the United States—letters of congratulations from Andrew Jackson and many other leaders proved that point—but he had no thought of a triumphant return to Tennessee. He remained committed to Texas and returned as quickly as he could, leaving New Orleans in mid-June and traveling by way of Natchitoches to San Augustine, where he attended a barbecue on July 4.

Affairs in Texas bordered on chaos. Burnet's government took Santa Anna from Galveston to Velasco at the mouth of the Brazos River and there, on May 14, they signed two treaties, one public and one secret. The first provided for an end to hostilities and the removal of all Mexican troops south of the Rio Grande. In the secret agreement, Santa Anna promised in return for his release to work for recognition of Texas's independence by Mexico. These treaties were in line with Houston's thinking. However, Secretary of War Lamar and Secretary of the Navy Potter refused to sign, indicating the disagreement with Houston's designs for peace that would soon become prevalent in the army and over-whelm Burnet's government. In early June—after Santa Anna, Almonte, and other officers had been put on board a ship at Velasco for the trip to Veracruz—recently arrived volunteers from the United States led by Thomas Jefferson Green and Memucan Hunt forced the government to remove the Mexicans and return them to prison. Hotheads continued to call for vengeance for the Alamo and Goliad. To protect Santa Anna from the mob spirit created by Green and Hunt, he was moved to Columbia about 20 miles upriver, and the government followed.

Burnet's problems with the Texas army increased during the summer of 1836 as it—having followed the retreating Mexicans to Victoria—became highly restive over having no one to fight and over reports that Santa Anna was to be released. Burnet sought to replace Rusk with Lamar as acting commander in chief, apparently with the intention of having a general of his own choice, even if Lamar did tend to side with the hotheads on how to deal with Santa Anna. The army, however, rejected Lamar on the grounds that he lacked the necessary qualifications, and Rusk remained in command. Later in July, Burnet, in another effort to placate the army, revived the idea of an offensive against Mata-moros.

Houston's reaction was predictable. He wrote to Rusk on July 26 expressing disbelief that the army intended to take revenge on Santa Anna. "Santa Anna living . . . may be of incalculable advantage to Texas in her present crisis," he wrote. But, "In cool blood to offer up the living to the names of the departed, only finds an example in the religion and warfare of Savages." Another letter on August 8 thoroughly condemned the Matamoros project. An offensive, he wrote, contains risks far greater than any advan-tage that could come from taking the city. "Our policy," he insisted, "is to hazard nothing — let us act on the defensive. . . . A wise man will wait for the harvest, and prepare the reapers for it when it comes." Burnet claimed that Houston was responsible for the unrest in the army, but in fact, exactly the opposite was true. The cautious commander had no intention of changing the approach that he had followed since fighting began in 1835, and he always insisted that the military subordinate itself to civilian authority.

Burnet's interim government was scheduled to operate until December 1836, but the president, desperate to find a way of bringing order to Texas, decided to hold elections and institute regular government ahead of schedule. On July 23 he issued a proclamation setting September 5 as the date Texans would vote on accepting the constitution written at the convention the previous March, elect officials under that constitution, and express opinions on annexation to the United States. The new republic had no formal political parties, so the contests for office promised to be largely personal. Henry Smith and Stephen F. Austin soon announced as candidates for the presidency. Smith had served as governor of the provisional state government set up by the Consultation in 1835 and eventually became so embroiled in controversy with the General Council that he was removed from office. He wanted vindication. Austin's qualifications were obvious, but many thought that he had been too slow in breaking with Mexico, and he had not been involved in the major military events of 1836, having served as a diplomat to the United States during the war.

Preferring to return to the army, Sam Houston did not seek a nomination for the presidency, but he had misgivings about both Smith and Austin. Moreover, many Texans urged Houston to run. A mass meeting in San Augustine on August 15 nominated him for president, and a nominating resolution sent from Columbia on August 23 had 600 signatures. Finally, two weeks before the election, Houston announced in a letter to George Hockley that he had "yielded to the wishes of my friends" because "the crisis requires it." Texas, he believed, had become so divided between adherents of Smith and Austin that a victory by either would create dangerous disunity in the republic. Houston thus saw himself as the candidate who could bring unity, and the results bore out his belief. He received 5,119 votes to 743 for Smith, who had announced his withdrawal once the hero of San Jacinto entered the contest, and 587 for Austin. Mirabeau B. Lamar, who was by no means a friend or political ally of the president-elect, won the vice presidency. Voters approved the constitution unanimously and sanctioned annexation to the United States by an overwhelming margin. Thus Texans, even as they established a government for their new republic, indicated that they would give up independence in order to become part of the nation where most had been born.

Soon after the election, interim president Burnet called the First Congress of the republic to meet at Columbia on October 3, 1836. Once the Congress had organized, he and interim vice-president Zavala resigned so that Houston and Lamar could be inaugurated. The new president's inaugural address, delivered on October 22, emphasized the problems facing the republic and the need for unity in dealing with them. "I am perfectly aware," he said, "of the difficulties that surround me. . . ." He called for vigilance in dealing with Mexico and a policy of fairness and peace toward the Indians. Reminding his listeners of the popular mandate that Texas "be reunited to the great Republican family of the North," he asked, "Will our friends disregard it?" Then, in conclusion, he removed his sword, calling it an "emblem of my past office," and promising to take it up again only in defense of his country. Whatever his critics may have feared, Sam Houston never considered military rule an acceptable alternative to constitutional government. At Columbia the Congress met in an unfinished shack, and the president worked in a one-room office heated by a fireplace. At first, he did not have a good copy of the Constitution or any archives—other than some papers thrown in a trunk—or an official seal or even a pen to sign commissions.

Houston's major cabinet appointments demonstrated his desire for unity. He made his defeated opponents Austin and Smith secretary of state and secretary of the treasury respectively, and attempted to conciliate Burnet by offering the position of attorney general to one of his supporters, James Collinsworth. This olive branch was refused, however, and James Pinckney Henderson became the first attorney general. Once the personnel of his administration were in place, the new president could give attention to the "difficulties" alluded to in his inaugural address. Mexico threatened to resume hostilities at any moment. The new republic had not received diplomatic recognition from any nation, not even the United States. The army had numerous adventurers—many of whom had arrived after San Jacinto—calling for Santa Anna's blood and an invasion of Mexico. There was a threat of trouble with the Indians unless the Cherokees in East Texas were secured in their land claims and peace could be arranged with the Comanches on the frontier. Finally, the republic had a debt of $1.25 million and an empty treasury. Houston wrestled with these problems for the slightly more than two years of his presidency, from October 22, 1836, to December 10, 1838.

The United States was the new republic's best friend, but President Houston found diplomatic recognition difficult to obtain. First, Mexico had not accepted the independence of Texas, and recognition by the United States would almost certainly mean trouble between the governments in Washington and Mexico City. President Andrew Jackson did not want a crisis with Mexico, especially since he was trying to settle claims that citizens of his nation had against the Mexican government. Second, antislavery activists in the United States, particularly Benjamin Lundy who had once hoped to colonize emancipated slaves in Texas—insisted that the revolution of 1835–1836 had resulted from a conspiracy to add more slave territory to the Union. John Quincy Adams, former president and now a congressman from Massachusetts, led the attack on Texas in Washington. With the election of 1836 set for early November, President Jackson and Vice President Martin Van Buren, who was running to succeed Old Hickory, did not want to create a controversy by granting recognition. Texas simply had to wait.

Although unable to gain quick recognition in the fall of 1836, Houston took several steps calculated at least in part to improve the chances of favorable action by the United States. At his urging, the Texas Congress passed a boundary act on December 19, encompassing as much of Mexico as possible. The southwestern boundary began at the mouth of the Rio Grande and followed the river to its source and thence due north to the 42nd parallel. Since Texas had never extended southwest of the Nueces River during the Spanish and Mexican periods, this definition, which gave the republic claims to half of New Mexico and lands stretching northward into Wyoming, was generous indeed. The other step involved Santa Anna, who had been an effective hostage while Mexican armies moved beyond the Rio Grande but now provided an inviting target for vengeful Texans. Houston, fearing that someone might kill the Mexican commander and thereby hurt Texas's chances of winning recognition as a civilized nation, proposed to send him home by way of Washington. "I now regard our national standing," the president told the Senate, "as connected with the preservation of his life." We are gaining no advantage by holding him longer, he argued, whereas gain "*may result*" if we allow him to visit President Jackson and then go on to Mexico. Houston hoped that recognition or perhaps even an arrangement allowing Texas to become part of the United States might result. In any case, Santa Anna would be safely out of the republic.

The Texas Congress claimed control of the Mexican dictator, but Houston argued that the "unrestricted powers" given him as commander in chief "confided to me the disposition of the prisoners." So, on November 25, 1836, George Hockley and two other trusted officers left Columbia for Washington with Santa Anna. Hockley carried a confidential letter from Houston to Jackson explaining that Santa Anna was being liberated "in accordance with your wishes" and that William H. Wharton was being sent to Washington as an official diplomatic representative of the new republic. "My great desire," he told Old Hickory, "is that our country Texas shall be annexed to the United States ... on a footing of Justice and reciprocity to [both] parties." Everyone there was of the opinion that our republic could stand against any power, he continued, "yet I am free to say *to you* that we cannot do it." In spite of the great victory at San Jacinto, Houston refused to be overconfident. As commander in chief and now as president, he was always the cautious realist.

Santa Anna's visit to Washington went smoothly. He met Jackson, talked unsuccessfully about the possibility of receiving "a few millions" from the United States for Texas, and sailed for Veracruz on a U.S. naval vessel. Once safely back in Mexico, Santa

Anna repudiated all the promises made in the Treaties of Velasco. Within a few years, he returned to control of the government and became once again a threat to Texas. Houston, however, had no illusions about the dictator's character and had performed a service simply by getting rid of him without disgracing the new republic.

The Christmas season in 1836 brought one discouragement after another on the diplomatic front. President Jackson's annual message, delivered on December 22, expressed the opinion that immediate recognition of Texas would be "impolitic." Five days later in Columbia, Secretary of State Stephen F. Austin, with whom Houston had developed a close working relationship in seeking recognition, died of pneumonia at the age of 43. "The Father of Texas is no more!" the president announced, as he ordered 30 days of official mourning throughout the republic. James Pinckney Henderson took Austin's place as secretary of state, and soon he and Houston were encouraged by the aggressive diplomacy of William H. Wharton in Washington. The agent from Texas told Jackson that the failure to grant immediate recognition denied Texas the opportunity to establish credit and secure itself financially and played into the hands of Mexico. The Mexicans, Wharton said, will have your annual message "printed on Satin and circulated throughout all the country." In response, Jackson indicated that if Congress recommended recognition he would concur immediately. Wharton then went to work on the Jacksonians in Congress, and the appropriations bill passed at the end of February 1837 contained funds to pay a diplomatic agent to Texas when the president decided to act. On March 3, just one day before his term ended, Jackson called in Wharton and Memucan Hunt, who had also been sent to represent Texas in Washington, and announced that he had nominated Alcée La Branche of Louisiana to be chargé d'affaires to Texas. They drank a toast to the independence of the republic.

Texans celebrated recognition, but with an undercurrent of disappointment that it had not included an offer to join the United States. Realistic men could see, as did William Fairfax Gray—who had carefully observed affairs since the convention in March 1836—that "Texas independent, and compelled to fight her own battles and pay her own debts, will necessarily have to impose heavy burdens [on] her citizens." The president's job was not likely to become any easier.

As Houston celebrated his forty-fourth birthday and the Republic of Texas its first on March 2, 1837, his personal life was little more settled than was the public life of his new nation. He remained a bachelor, living under miserable conditions at Columbia, and he wanted a change. If I could just see my country at peace, he wrote Irion, I would retire to East Texas, "get a fair, sweet 'wee wifie,' as Burns says, and pass the balance of my sinful life in ease and comfort, (if I can)." Clearly the "wifie" of his dreams remained Anna Raguet, the young woman whom he had met in Nacogdoches in 1833. On the day after San Jacinto, he had sent her a wreath of laurel leaves—the "laurels" of victory—and his courtship continued after he became president. "I will not marry," he wrote her in January 1837, "until I can once more go to Nacogdoches and see how my matters are there!" In April of that year, the republic moved its capital to a new "city" on Buffalo Bayou named Houston by its promoter-builders, Augustus C. and John K. Allen. The president expressed unhappiness to his friend Irion that "the fair Miss Anna" would not be there because, he wrote with wonderful double entendre, "she has a great aversion to 'Houston.'" Lamenting how sad the scene would be at social events where he would have no "Mrs. H___," while others would "claim fair Dames as theirs!!!" he concluded, "My day may come!"

In Houston the president lived and worked in a log cabin of two rooms separated by a covered breezeway or "dog trot." He continued to emphasize the desirability of annexation to the United States, telling the first congress to assemble in the new capital that Texas's attitude on the subject had not changed and to hope for action by the next session of the United States Congress in Washington. On August 4, 1837, Memucan Hunt, who had succeeded Wharton as minister to the United States, made a formal proposal of annexation to the administration of Martin Van Buren. Secretary of State John Forsyth quickly rejected the offer on the grounds, recently brought up by John Quincy Adams, that it was unconstitutional to annex an independent foreign territory and that it would involve the United States in Texas's war with Mexico. Van Buren did not need trouble over Texas, either at home or abroad, especially since a serious financial panic had hit the United States earlier in 1837. Houston accepted this rebuff quietly, but in May 1838 he instructed Hunt to withdraw the annexation request. Formal withdrawal took place in October 1838. The republic's new minister, Anson Jones, wrote: "How *glorious* will Texas be standing alone, and relying upon her own strength." More than likely, Houston's reaction to this statement would have been a wry smile.

The president knew that if Texas did not become part of the United States the republic had to build friendly relations with the great powers of Europe. Accordingly, in June 1837, he appointed James Pinckney Henderson minister to Great Britain and France with the task of gaining recognition, commercial treaties, and financial aid. Henderson found the British friendly but unwilling to act, probably because they did not want to antagonize Mexico, did not like slavery in Texas, and thought the new republic likely to join the United States soon. He then went on to France, where because that nation was on the verge of war with Mexico, his reception was even friendlier than in London, but recognition was not forthcoming there either. Thus Houston achieved only one diplomatic success—recognition by the United States—during his first administration from October 1836 to December 1838.

While dealing with these foreign policy issues, the president also faced serious internal difficulties. The army, the scene of so much trouble for Burnet, remained full of hotheads who wanted to mount an offensive against Mexico. In October 1836, Houston made Rusk, who had taken command after San Jacinto, his secretary of war and appointed General Felix Huston to take Rusk's place. Much to the president's disgust, Huston began to advocate the Matamoros scheme that had plagued military efforts in Texas since late 1835. In January 1837, Houston appointed Albert Sidney Johnston, a West Point–trained officer of great ability, to replace Huston in command of the army. Huston, however, saw this as an insult to his honor, challenged Johnston to a duel, and inflicted a serious wound on the would-be replacement commander. Then, in May 1837, he left the army of more than 2,000 men at San Antonio under the temporary command of a friend, and went to the capital to promote his scheme for an attack on Matamoros. His promises of glory for Texas and spoils to pay the republic's debts received a favorable hearing from Congress and prompted Houston to an act that critics probably would have called "Indian cunning." The president invited General Huston to stay at the executive's home, lulled him into complacency, and, while he slept, had the secretary of war go to San Antonio and give 30-day furloughs to all the troops except 600 men. Those who received furloughs were sent to various points along the Gulf coast, after being told that upon their return there was much hard work such as draining marshes and building railroads to be done. When Huston returned to the army and discovered the results of what one observer called this "judicious system of furloughing," he left for the United States. Texas's armed forces were rebuilt, but with fewer hotheads and adventurers. Once more, Houston had prevented a foolish campaign against Matamoros and demonstrated his belief that peace and a defensive posture offered the only hope for the republic's survival.

Ironically, while some wanted to continue the war against Mexico, a much greater threat of violence to Texans came from Indians on the frontier. In May 1836, for example, more than 500 Comanches and Kiowas attacked Parker's Fort in Limestone County, killing the defenders and taking women and children as prisoners. With little money and numerous problems, the Houston administration could do little about the Comanches and other tribes along the frontier, although, beginning in 1837, the use of mounted forces that ranged between fortified positions offered some protection to settlers. Indian warfare in the West would continue well beyond the years of the republic.

The Cherokees of East Texas presented a different kind of problem, with especially upsetting results for Houston. The treaty he had signed with them in February 1836, which promised respect for their land claims in return for neutrality in the war, had not been ratified by the convention or by the interim government. Houston submitted it to the Texas Senate in December 1836 and urged ratification, calling it "just and equitable." The Senate, however, encouraged by Vice President Lamar, delayed through most of 1837 and finally refused to ratify it on several grounds, including the charge that the Indians had not kept their part of the bargain. In essence, of course, the story was a familiar one—settlers wanted the Cherokees' land. New treaty negotiations initiated by Houston failed, and then in 1838 the president's desire for peace and fair treatment of the Indians received a serious blow when they were implicated in an abortive rebellion against the republic. This uprising was the work of Vicente Córdova, a Mexican resident of Nacogdoches, who brought together on the Angelina River in August 1838 a force of Mexicans and Indians estimated at 400 to 600 men, and sent Houston a letter disclaiming allegiance to the Republic of Texas. The president called out a militia force, under the command of Thomas J. Rusk, which defeated the rebels in a battle at Kickapoo Village in mid-October. Córdova and other leaders escaped to Mexico, but Rusk marched to the village of the main Cherokee chief, Duwali (the Bowl), intending apparently to punish the tribe for their part in the rebellion. Duwali insisted that his people had nothing to do with Córdova, and the extent of Cherokee involvement in the rebellion has never been proven conclusively. Houston, who had written letter after letter to Duwali urging peace, pardoned all the Indians—Cherokees and other tribes alike—for any involvement they may have had with Córdova. Conflict ended for the moment, but within a year developments would destroy the hope that Houston expressed to Duwali in August 1838: "My brother. Be at peace and tell my red brothers to do so."

Land policy created yet another difficult problem. Texas's millions of acres constituted its primary resource for attracting settlers, rewarding soldiers, and raising money. Beginning with the Constitution of 1836, which promised every head of family in Texas at that time a league (4,428.4 acres) and a labor (177 acres) and every single man one-third of a league, the government of the republic gave away literally millions of acres. This policy meant that a huge number of surveys and claims had to be recorded, so Congress in December 1836 created a General Land Office "to superintend, execute, and perform all acts touching or respecting the public lands of Texas." Houston vetoed the act on the grounds that it did not establish clear rules for determining what land was already held by valid title and what was vacant—thereby creating confusion and inviting numerous legal actions—and that it would create a speculative mania as Texans, old and new, rushed to make claims. Congress passed the act over his veto, but he delayed as long as he could before appointing a commissioner and opening the General Land Office in October 1837. Houston was largely correct about the problems that would result from the act passed in 1836. Overlapping claims and land fraud would lead to constant litigation and, in some cases, even violence.

Finally, Houston faced seemingly insurmountable problems in financial policy. When he became president, the republic had a debt of $1.25 million and no effective way to raise money. Texans were generally too cash-poor to be taxed, and tariff duties, which were levied first in December 1836, brought in only a little revenue. So much land was being given away that it could not be sold as a source of income. The government attempted to borrow by passing a bill in the spring of 1837 that authorized the issuance of $5 million in bonds, but buyers were not available in the United States because of the Panic of 1837. By early June 1837, President Houston was ready to turn to the final resort—paper money. He informed Congress that he and other individuals in the government had used their own credit to buy supplies for the army and that no public official had been paid during his administration. You must be aware, he said, "of the absolute necessity of some provisions being made to sustain the country." Congress responded with the authorization of $500,000 in paper money, payable in specie one year after the issue and bearing interest at 10 percent. These notes were backed by the "full faith and credit of the government" and could be used to pay debts to the government, so they did not depreciate immediately. Nevertheless, during the remainder of Houston's administration, as the government's financial status did not improve and additional issues pushed the amount of paper in circulation to more than $800,000, its value began to decline. Texas paper money fell by late 1838 to about 65 cents on the United States dollar. This was not promising, but the paper money debacle was only beginning.

Beset on all sides by the problems that he had anticipated,

Houston worked long hours under terrible circumstances through 1837 and 1838. "It is late at night," he wrote Anna Raguet on February 1, 1838, "and I am freezing in a miserable open house; four windows in it, and not one pane of glass or shutter—three doors, and shutters to but two—no ceiling and the floor loose laid. Is this not a 'White House' with a plague to it?" Meanwhile, his personal life remained as unsettled as affairs in the republic. His weakness for alcohol had not disappeared, as witnessed by a friendly bet (a $500 suit of clothes) with Augustus C. Allen on January 7, 1837, that he would not drink anything other than "malt liquors" for the next year. The winner of this bet is unknown.

Houston continued his courtship of Anna Raguet without success. She was 22 in 1838, had many suitors, and clearly had reservations about a much-older man with such a questionable past. Above all, there was the matter of Houston's marriage to Eliza Allen. He had filed for divorce in 1833, but the final decree was not given until 1837. When Anna heard of the divorce, she complained that Houston should not have "addressed" her while married to another. He responded in June 1838 by telling her that he had believed himself "free from all legal or moral hindrance to any union which might be created" and that he still "merited the esteem with which you have honored me in by gone days." She did not respond to his appeal and would not become his bride. His friend, Robert A. Irion, who was thirteen years younger and also a suitor for her hand, won the prize in April 1840. Houston remained on good terms with both, and the couple named their eldest son Sam Houston Irion.

The Constitution limited the term of the first president to two years, December 1836 to December 1838, and made him ineligible for reelection. Therefore, Texans had no opportunity to express directly at the polls their views on Houston's administration. With the president ineligible to run and no strong candidate to represent him, victory went to anti-Houston men, Mirabeau B. Lamar and David G. Burnet. Lamar appealed especially to western areas by promising a tougher stance against the Mexicans and Indians, but he also promised to improve the republic's finances and have Texas continue to stand on its own as an independent nation. Houston and his friends tried unsuccessfully to convince Thomas Jefferson Rusk to run and then turned to Peter W. Grayson, the attorney general. However, their candidate committed suicide during a fit of depression in July, whereupon they nominated James Collinsworth, the chief justice of the Texas Supreme Court. Within a month this second candidate also killed himself by leaping while drunk from a steamboat into Galveston Bay. The Houston party finally selected Robert Wilson, a little-known senator, who came into the race late without any chance of winning. Lamar won by a margin of 6,995 to 252, and Burnet took the vice presidency.

Lamar's inauguration on December 1, 1838, offered the outgoing president one last chance to defend his record against those who wished to repudiate it. He appeared in knee breeches with silver buckles, a silk coat, and a powdered wig—an outfit better suited to the days of George Washington than to Texas in the 1830s—and proceeded to make a "Farewell Address" that continued for three hours. Indulging in every oratorical trick imaginable, he regaled the audience with a wildly exaggerated account of how difficult and successful his presidency had been. Finally, Houston turned the stage over to Lamar, who had spent much time preparing what he considered a literary masterpiece among inaugural addresses, but the new president had become so upset by the preceding performance that he was unable to deliver his speech. It was read by his private secretary.

Houston's presidency had brought significant progress, but the infant republic remained far from secure. Establishing a successful government in a huge, sparsely populated new nation presented problems too great to solve in two years. Texas still needed the ex-president's political leadership.

CHAPTER SEVEN

"The Only Man for Texas"

❖
❖

In December 1838, Houston found himself out of public service for the first time in three years, and he seemed to welcome the change. He formed a law partnership in Houston with John Birdsall—a native New Yorker who had served as the second chief justice of the Republic of Texas—and also joined several of his old friends, including George W. Hockley, in promoting the development of a new town at the mouth of the Sabine River. The promoters named their project Sabine City and promised that it would become the commercial center for all of southeast Texas between the Trinity River and Louisiana. This venture in city building needed investment capital from the United States. In the spring of 1839 Houston undertook a trip to New Orleans, Mobile, and Nashville to interest investors in Sabine City, buy horses for a ranch he was developing at Grand Cane on the Trinity, and visit Andrew Jackson, whom he had not seen since 1834.

Houston visited his friend, William Christy, in New Orleans and went on to Mobile, where he sought to interest a wealthy merchant named William Bledsoe in the Sabine City project. The ex-president accepted an invitation to visit the Bledsoe estate near Mobile, and there he met Margaret Lea, the 20year-old sister of the host's wife. Once again, Houston was immediately attracted to a beautiful younger woman. According to family legend, he at first mistook her for Bledsoe's wife and commented to another guest that if she were not married he would give her a chance to say no. Informed that Margaret Lea was the unmarried sister, he immediately expressed his interest and happily found that she had followed news of his career and hoped to meet him.

Houston spent a week at Bledsoe's, winning Margaret for himself and for Texas. One evening, with perfect symbolism, he pointed to a lone star low in the darkening sky and told her that it was their star of destiny, to think of it when he was not there. He went on to visit Jackson, who was living in retirement at the Hermitage, but his thoughts concentrated on Margaret. A letter that he wrote to her soon after reaching Nashville drew a very encouraging response; the first letter, she said, "I have addressed to any gentleman." "Last night," she continued, "I gazed long upon our beauteous emblem the *star of destiny*, and my thoughts took the form of verse. . . ." Houston returned to Alabama in August 1839, visited the Leas' home, and received a promise that Margaret's widowed mother, Nancy Lea, and her son-in-law, William Bledsoe, would visit Texas the next spring to look over possible land investments. He assumed that Margaret would accompany them and left for home in September believing himself engaged and soon to be wed.

Upon returning to East Texas, Houston found that voters in San Augustine had chosen him their representative in the Fourth Congress of the republic scheduled to meet in December 1839. This proved to be a welcome opportunity to return to public life because, to his way of thinking, many of the policies instituted by President Lamar during his first year in office were utterly wrong and deserved opposition. For one thing, Congress, at Lamar's urging, had moved the capital from Houston to a tiny hamlet on the Colorado River called Waterloo. The government relocated to Austin, the new name for the town, in October 1839, and Houston would have to attend the first session of Congress there. Having the capital removed from his namesake city was a blow to Houston's pride, but he objected also because Austin's location on the western edge of Anglo settlement in Texas exposed it to attacks by Comanches and Mexicans.

If moving the capital irritated Houston, Lamar's policy toward the Cherokees infuriated the ex-president. The Indians' title to their lands in Texas had remained in doubt when Houston left office because Congress would not ratify the treaty that he had signed with Duwali and other chiefs in February 1836. In his first message to Congress, Lamar denied that the Cherokees had any legitimate land titles from Mexico or the republic and indicated that they could either accept Texas law, which would open their lands to settlers, or move, or be destroyed. Congress backed this belligerent stand, and by the spring of 1839 the government found an excuse for war. In May, Manuel Flores and a band of Cherokees were intercepted by Texans as they attempted to cross the Colorado River near the future site of Austin. Papers taken from Flores's body showed that he was representing the government of Mexico in a plot to create a general uprising of the Cherokees, and in reaction President Lamar sent troops onto the lands claimed by the Indians. There were attempts to negotiate a removal of the Cherokees from the republic, but the Texans, fearing that delay would mean help from Mexico, attacked. The Battle of the Neches, fought near present-day Tyler in mid-July 1839, resulted in total victory for Lamar's forces. Duwali was killed, scalped, and a sword that Houston had given him in 1836 taken from his body. Those Indians who survived were driven into the Indian Territory to the north of Texas.

Most Texans supported Lamar's aggressive Indian policy, but Houston was outraged. Before leaving for the meeting of Congress in Austin, he spoke at Nacogdoches and denounced the attack on the Cherokees in language that angered even his closest friends. Once Congress assembled, Houston—after venting his spleen against the relocation of the capital—returned to the Indian question in speech after speech. The Cherokees, he said, had never drawn one drop of a white man's blood, but the government had treated them with duplicity and fraud and had unjustifiably driven them from their homes and land. Houston's enemies responded angrily, and Edward Burleson, who had fought in the Battle of the Neches, fanned the flames by sending him the hat that Duwali had worn there. This insult provoked another lengthy speech in which Houston charged that the government's Indian policy was formulated to aid speculators such as Vice President Burnet in grabbing Cherokee lands.

Although Houston stood virtually alone on questions of Indian policy—his behavior, the *Houston Telegraph and Texas*

Register said, "excited the grief and shame of his friends, and the just reproach and scorn of his enemies"—he nevertheless found a shrewd way to gain popular support for his argument that the Cherokees' land claims had been valid. On December 22, 1839, he introduced a bill providing for surveying "the lands lately *owned* and occupied by the Cherokee Indians" into 640-acre tracts to be sold with the proceeds going to the government. The Indians had owned the land, he argued, so the government by virtue of conquest could sell it. Congressmen, unless they wanted to deny the public an opportunity to purchase land and the treasury a financial gain, had to go along with this bill, which acknowledged the Indians' legal title and, at the same time, prevented speculators from snapping up huge tracts. The bill passed almost unanimously in January 1840. Although Congress repealed it the next year, Houston nevertheless gained a little revenge for the fate of the Cherokees.

Houston's service in the Fourth Congress in 1839 to 1840 marked a major step toward dividing politically active citizens of the republic into Houston and anti-Houston parties. In a sense this division had existed since 1835, when Houston disagreed with the war party leaders on an immediate declaration of independence from Mexico, but Lamar's attack on the record of his first administration and his response made party lines much clearer. Through the remaining years of the republic, and to a large extent for the rest of his life, views of Houston and his policies constituted a major basis for political divisions in Texas.

The end of the Fourth Congress in February 1840 coincided with the expected arrival in Texas of Margaret Lea with her mother and brother-in-law, William Bledsoe. Houston went to Galveston to meet her ship but found only Mrs. Lea and Bledsoe on board. When he inquired as to Margaret's whereabouts, Nancy Lea replied: "General Houston, my daughter is in Alabama. She goes forth in the world to marry no man. The one who receives her hand will receive it in my home and not elsewhere." Houston promptly surrendered to this demand. He and Margaret Lea were married in Marion, Alabama, on May 9, 1840; she was 21 and he was 47. The newlyweds returned to Texas by way of New Orleans and Galveston, visited in the Nacogdoches area, and settled at first in Houston. Many, including some of the groom's best friends, thought the marriage a mistake, but it proved a blessing. Painfully aware of his weakness for alcohol, Margaret persuaded him to stop excessive drinking and in a few years convinced him to join the Baptist Church. Sam Houston, Jr., the first of a family of eight, was born in 1843, when Houston was 50. At last, he had the wife and family that he had wanted for years.

Houston, having been reelected in September 1840, again represented the San Augustine district when the Fifth Congress assembled in Austin in December. The republic, now approaching its third year under Lamar's leadership, had more difficulties than ever. For one thing, the president's aggressive Indian policy had extended to the Comanches as well as the Cherokees but with far less decisive results. A meeting between Texas peace commissioners and Comanche chiefs at the Council House in San Antonio in March 1840 had turned into a fight in which 35 Indians and 7 Texans were killed. Then, in August, the Comanches had raided past San Antonio all the way to the coast, attacking Victoria and Linnville, before being defeated at Plum Creek by a Texas force under·Edward Burleson, Felix Huston, and Ben McCulloch. Although there would be no further conflict with the Comanches for the next few years, these events created fear and slowed settlement on the frontier.

Lamar's financial policies upset more Texans than did his aggressiveness toward the Indians. Having inherited the use of paper money and a debt of about $2 million from Houston, the new administration printed and spent at such a rate that in three years the debt reached $7 million, more than triple its level in 1838. The public lost confidence in the republic's paper money to the point that it stood at 12 to 15 cents on the United States dollar by late 1841.

The Lamar administration had achieved several major diplomatic triumphs during its first two years—recognition by and a commercial treaty with France in 1839 and similar arrangements with Great Britain and Holland in 1840—but in spite of repeated efforts it had not reached any sort of diplomatic settlement with Mexico. No Mexican government could sign a peace treaty and grant recognition to Texas without being ruined by the negative public reaction at home. Mexico's official position remained, in the words of a Veracruz newspaper, that there is no "republic of Texas," only "a horde of adventurers in rebellion against the laws of the government of the republic." Frustrated, Lamar in December 1840 asked Congress for a declaration of war against Mexico. Houston successfuly opposed this with the sensible argument that, rather than going to war because it could not negotiate peace, Texas needed to avoid conflict and use the time to build its strength. Lamar then proposed an expedition to Santa Fe to make good the republic's claim—implied in the public Treaty of Velasco and stated in the Boundary Act of 1836—to the eastern half of New Mexico. The Texans would present themselves as a peace mission seeking to establish commercial relations, but they would be accompanied by troops and carry plans for the establishment of a territorial government. Houston immediately attacked this scheme for being dangerously beyond the republic's capabilities and likely to invite retaliation from Mexico. Congress refused to authorize the Santa Fe expediton, but Lamar remained determined to try it anyway.

A few weeks later, Lamar went to New Orleans for medical attention, and Vice President Burnet, upon becoming the acting president, renewed the call for an attack on Mexico. Houston again argued that Texas needed to strengthen itself at home rather than pursue foreign conquests. The House of Representatives postponed action on a declaration of war, but the wrangling became so bitter that the whole legislative session accomp-lished nothing. "We have been in session for months," Houston wrote Anthony Butler on February 2, 1841, "and little of advantage has resulted to our country from the session. We are in a bad box, and I fear it is locked upon us!" He blamed Lamar and Burnet for the problem and claimed that it would require great effort to restore the republic to the situation their administration inherited in 1838.

Interest in the presidential election scheduled for September 6 ran high from the beginning of the year. Lamar could not succeed himself, but Vice President Burnet intended to run, and that set up a perfect match between Houston and his most dedicated enemy. Although there were plenty of issues to debate—public finance, Indian policy, location of the capital, and the land distribution system, for example—the contest immediately became personal. Burnet called Houston a drunken half-Indian, notable only for his cowardice at San Jacinto. Houston in turn ridiculed Burnet as "Little Davy" and called him a "hog thief." Enraged, the vice president challenged Houston to a duel, but the latter laughed it off on several grounds, including a claim that he "never fought downhill." During the summer the two candidates took their personal battle into the newspapers, Burnet charging Houston with "beastly intemperance and other vices degrading to humanity" and being called in return a "political brawler and canting hypocrite, whom the waters of Jordon could never cleanse from your political and moral leprosy."

Houston's campaign against Burnet in the summer of 1841 was made more difficult by personal circumstances. Margaret suffered a great deal with respiratory problems, so in July they moved to a partially finished home at Cedar Point on Galveston Bay, where she could breathe the salt air. Her health improved, but the move was costly, and Houston was in financial difficulty anyhow. He had spent much of his time on politics rather than law, and the republic's poor financial condition hurt, too. Moreover, two slave boys for whom he had paid $2,100 ran away to Mexico. In late July, he was reduced to asking Samuel May Williams for a loan of $60 or $80 and telling an old friend in Tennessee that he could not repay a previous loan of $500.

Houston gained political and personal vindication on September 6 by defeating Burnet 7,508 votes to 2,574. The great majority of Texans apparently agreed with the view expressed by James Morgan back in January: "Old Sam H. with all his faults appears to be the only man for Texas—He is still unsteady, intemperate, but drunk in a ditch is worth a thousand of Lamar and Burnet." Had he been better informed, Morgan might have raised the number because the president-elect had greatly reduced his drinking. A huge victory celebration in Washington County was, in the words of one observer, a "cold water *doins*," for the guest of honor did not touch the "smallest drop of the ardent during his stay in this county." During October and November, Houston accepted congratulations, made speeches promising changes in current policies, and put together a cabinet led by Anson Jones as secretary of state. Then, leaving Margaret in East Texas to spare her the strain of a trip to Austin, he headed for Lamar's capital, where he was inaugurated on December 13, 1841.

Houston devoted his inaugural address to attacking the Lamar administration, so Texans had to wait until his message to Congress on December 20 for a list of specific recommendations on policy changes. He began with a warning that the republic had reached a crisis that was "neither cheering for the present nor flattering for the future" and then focused on three main problem areas—finance, Indian policy, and relations with Mexico. Finance presented the greatest difficulties. "We have no money," he told Congress. "We cannot redeem our liabilities." In this situation, he recommended suspending all payments of interest and principal on the public debt, limiting use of paper money to a new issue of $350,000 that could be used at par to pay all debts to the government, and borrowing $300,000 that would be backed by designated public lands. Turning to Indian policy, the new president urged a drastic change—from war to peace—by signing treaties that would establish boundaries between Texan settlements and Indian lands and by licensing everyone who traded with the tribes or went into their country. Where Mexico was concerned, Houston pointed out that diplomatic relations had not improved since 1836 and recommended leaving the Mexican nation alone. Civil unrest will weaken Mexico, he argued, while emigration from the United States will give Texas the power to withstand aggression. Houston began his second term in typically cautious fashion by advocating financial retrenchment, pacification of the Indians, and peace with Mexico.

Congress enthusiastically embraced the president's proposals for tightening the republic's purse strings, in some cases advancing stringency even beyond his recommendations. Payments on the public debt were suspended, and no effort was made to borrow more money. The government issued only $200,000 in paper money, a new type of "exchequer bill" that could be used to pay taxes and custom duties. Salaries paid to public officials were reduced; the president, for example, saw his pay cut from $10,000 to $5,000; and many government jobs were simply abolished. Military expenditures were greatly reduced as well.

Houston's second administration cost approximately $500,000, whereas Lamar had spent nearly $5 million, and the republic operated with an almost balanced budget by 1844. Nevertheless, its paper money continued to circulate at depreciated rates, and the public debt, with no interest or principal being paid, grew to $12 million by 1846. Houston's second administration went a long way toward stabilizing Texas's finances, but serious problems remained.

Congress also generally supported proposals for pacifying the Indians through negotiations and the establishment of licensed trading posts. In 1842, trading posts were authorized along the frontier at points such as San Marcos and Waco, and the next year saw the creation of the Bureau of Indian Affairs to regulate those commercial operations. Negotiations with nine sedentary tribes at Bird's Fort on the upper Trinity in North Texas resulted in a September 1843 treaty calling for peace and the establishment of trading posts in that area. Finally, in October 1844, Houston met personally with representatives of the Comanches and ten other tribes in a council at the Falls of the Brazos and signed a treaty providing for peace and commerce with the most warlike Indians in Texas. Houston's policy largely ended white-Indian conflict in the republic. There would be no lasting peace until Anglos controlled all of Texas, but for the moment an end to the fighting saved lives and money and probably served the republic far better than did Lamar's belligerent approach.

Houston thus had no great difficulty in obtaining congressional cooperation on financial and Indian policy, but gaining support for his cautious approach to relations with Mexico proved quite another matter. Many Texans welcomed any excuse for conflict with Mexicans, and just as Houston began his second administration, former president Lamar's Santa Fe expedition gave the belligerent element an excellent opportunity to demand action. Congress, with Houston leading, had refused to approve Lamar's scheme for sending a military/commercial force that would "invite" the supposedly very willing people of Santa Fe to join the Republic of Texas. Nevertheless, Lamar went ahead with the expedition, sending four official commissioners and a party of soldiers, traders, and adventurers toward New Mexico during June 1841. Leaving from a camp near Austin, the expedition finally reached the vicinity of Tucumcari in October, totally worn out from travel through rough country, lack of food, and skirmishes with the Indians. Mexican troops forced the Texans to surrender without firing a shot, and the prisoners were then marched overland to Mexico City, a distance of more than 1,000 miles, and held in Perote Prison until April 1842.

When the fate of the Santa Fe expedition became known in Austin, outrage swept through Congress. Houston prevented a declaration of war against Mexico, but the legislature passed a ridiculous bill redefining the republic's boundaries to include all of the land south of the 42nd parallel and west of Texas to the Pacific Ocean plus the northern two-thirds of Mexico! It would have made Texas larger than the United States at that time. Houston called this bill a "legislative jest" and vetoed it, only to have Congress override his veto in February 1842. Nothing came of these wild boundary claims, but the Santa Fe expedition and its aftermath helped undermine the president's efforts to avoid trouble with Mexico.

The Texas navy under the command of Commodore Edwin W. Moore created additional difficulties in relations with the Mexican government. During Lamar's administration, the Texans' six ships had become involved in the continuing contest between centralists and federalists in Mexico, even to the point of taking money for aiding federalist forces in Yucatán. In the fall of 1841, an agreement was reached whereby the federalists were to pay the Texas navy $8,000 a month so long as at least three ships helped in the fight against the centralists. Knowing that Houston would oppose this provocative involvement in Mexican affairs, Commodore Moore left Galveston for the coast of Yucatán on inauguration day in December 1841. The new president sent recall orders immediately, but Moore managed to stay ahead of the messenger until March 1842 and then obeyed slowly. Thus the Texas navy joined the Santa Fe expedition in causing trouble with Mexico just as Houston sought to prevent conflict.

Congress adjourned on February 5, 1842, and Houston left immediately to join Margaret in his namesake city. He found many Texans still enraged over the treatment of the Santa Fe expedition prisoners and demanding an attack on Mexico. With considerable patience, he explained the difficulties of attacking Mexico City, the probability that an attempt to rescue the prisoners would lead to their execution, and the futility of angry threats. "The true interest of Texas," he wrote a group of Galveston citizens on March 3, "is to maintain peace with all nations and to cultivate her soil." Within a few days, however, Mexico invaded Texas for the first time since 1836, and Houston faced even greater difficulty in attempting to avoid war.

The Mexican government, again under the control of Santa Anna, needed no excuse to attack, but the invasion was at least partially in response to the Santa Fe expedition and the actions of the Texas navy. General Rafael Vásquez crossed the Rio Grande on March 5 with 1,400 men and quickly took San Antonio. He withdrew two days later, taking 100 prisoners back to Mexico. In response, Vice President Edward Burleson organized three companies of mounted volunteers and led them to San Antonio, apparently with the intention of pursuing Vásquez. Houston issued a general call to arms, but he meant to keep Texan forces under the command of regularly chosen officers and avoid an offensive war. He ordered General Alexander Somervell, commander of the republic's forces on the frontier, to take charge of all troops arriving at San Antonio. Many of the volunteers under Burleson would not accept Somervell as their commanding officer, but the vice president did not want to go against Houston's orders. While Burleson hesitated, Vásquez's army crossed the Rio Grande, and many of the volunteers became disgusted and went home.

The invasion in March 1842 greatly complicated Houston's policy toward Mexico because, in addition to facing new pressures for an offensive war, he had to prepare to defend the republic against another attack. Taking a strong stand and preparing for defensive war without at the same time encouraging those who wanted to invade Mexico proved delicate and difficult. Houston began by calling a special session of Congress to meet in the city of Houston on June 27. Texans from western counties grumbled that this amounted to a de facto relocation of the capital, but a quorum was present to hear his message on the opening day.

After reviewing recent problems with Mexico, the president raised the question of "aggressive warfare" and pointed out that the decision rested with Congress. But then he quickly added that if the lawmakers thought it "unwise or impracticable to invade Mexico," they could, at much less expense, allow the president to raise and maintain a force to defend the frontier. Houston hoped to ease war fever and yet build Texas's defenses.

Houston also addressed the republic's finances, pointing out that, although the government could not exist without revenue, Congress had virtually ended direct taxation and not permitted him to sell the Cherokee lands. Finally, he returned to a favorite subject, the relocation of the capital. The recent invasion had proven that Austin was too exposed to the enemy, he said; the seat of government should be moved to a more secure and convenient location.

Congress quickly destroyed Houston's hope that it might join him in easing the agitation for war. Instead, hotheaded legislators passed a bill declaring war on Mexico and authorizing the president to draft one-third of the adult male population, sell 10 million acres of land to raise funds, and personally lead the army across the Rio Grande. When Houston hesitated to sign the bill and reminded Congress that nothing had been done to stabilize finances or protect the frontier, outraged Texans threatened his life. He waited until July 22, the day before Congress was scheduled to adjourn, and sent in a veto message. His reasoning was simple—Texas did not have the means to put the necessary army into the field and support it. "Resources are one thing," he wrote, "means are another." He also argued that the bill gave nearly dictatorial powers to the president, a dangerous precedent in a free country. The veto momentarily increased the furor among hotheads who wanted war at any cost, but Congress adjourned without voting to override, and the crisis gradually passed. From the Hermitage, Andrew Jackson offered his congratulations on saving Texas from "folly and madness." The message should have evoked a wry smile from Houston because virtually all of those who were condemning him so angrily regarded Old Hickory as a great hero.

Having gained a little breathing space in dealing with Mexico,

Houston again turned his attention to the issue of relocating the capital. His namesake city had not been popular as a site for the recent special session, and after a new Congress (the seventh) was elected on September 5, 1842, he accepted the advice of friends and offered a compromise. Leaders in Washington-on-the-Brazos had earlier proposed their town for capital of the republic. Now, in early September, Houston accepted and ordered the government to move there for the fall meeting of Congress. Relocation would not be complete, however, until the republic's archives had been moved to the capital, and the citizens of Austin were ready to fight rather than part with the government's papers. One frontiersman dared Houston to complete moving the capital. "Truth is," he wrote, "that you are afeard you Dam old drunk Cherokee. We . . . would shoot you and every dam waggoner that you could start with the papers."

Houston always insisted that Austin was not secure against attack from Mexico, and on September 11, 1842, one day after he ordered the government to Washington-on-the-Brazos, a Mexican army under General Adrián Woll swept into Texas and captured San Antonio. Any satisfaction the president may have gained from another demonstration of Austin's vulnerability, however, quickly faded in the face of renewed demands for an offensive war against Mexico. Volunteers and a small force of rangers commanded by Captain John C. "Jack" Hays rushed to San Antonio and lured the Mexican army into a battle on Salado Creek just to the east of the city. The Texans defeated Woll but allowed him to retreat into the city and then to head back to Mexico on September 18. Houston ordered three companies of militia to San Antonio and once again gave command to General Alexander Somervell, authorizing him to pursue Woll's army to the Rio Grande and, if there was "a prospect of success," to invade Mexico. Texans at last had their offensive war, although Houston did not give the order until October 3, more than two weeks after the Mexicans left San Antonio, and probably hoped that delay would allow this crisis to pass also.

If the president wanted delay, Somervell was the perfect commander. His 800-man army did not leave San Antonio until November 25 and took more than two weeks to reach Laredo, approximately 150 miles to the southwest. Finding no Mexican troops there, Somervell moved his army—already reduced by about 200 men who went home when he forced them to return property they stole from the people of Laredo—down the Rio Grande to a spot opposite the town of Guerrero. After forcing the citizens of Guerrero to provide food and clothing, many of the Texans wanted to cross into Mexico and conduct an offensive war while living off the land. Somervell hesitated and then, on December 19, ordered a retreat toward Gonzales. However, about 300 men refused to obey, chose Colonel William S. Fisher as their commander, and decided to continue the campaign.

Fisher and his men moved on down the Rio Grande to Mier, crossed the river, and entered the town without opposition. They demanded supplies and money, took the alcalde (the town's chief judicial and executive official) hostage to ensure delivery, and went back across the river to wait. Almost immediately, General Pedro de Ampudia occupied Mier with an army of more than 900 men. When Fisher learned of the arrival of Mexican troops, he decided to attack without first ascertaining how large a force he faced. The battle began on Christmas Day and continued into the twenty-sixth before the Texans, running short of ammunition and supplies, surrendered. Fisher and his men were marched toward Mexico City. South of Saltillo in February 1843, they escaped their guards, only to be recaptured as they headed northward through the Mexican desert. As retribution for the deaths of 5 Mexican soldiers killed in the escape attempt, Santa Anna ordered the execution of one in every ten of the 176 men still alive. The Mexicans put 159 white beans and 17 black beans in a pot and forced the Texans to draw. The 17 who drew black beans were blindfolded and shot on March 25, 1843, and the survivors continued the march to Perote Prison about 160 miles inland from Veracruz.

As news of the fate of the so-called Mier Expedition filtered back into Texas, Houston once again came under pressure to attack Mexico. He responded, almost wearily it seems, by pointing out that Fisher had not been given authority to cross the Rio Grande and that anything but a defensive war was foolish. "You will admit," he wrote George W. Hockley in May 1843 concerning the demand for an invasion, "that but one foolery is stationary with us, and that is *to make war without means*." Houston did what he could for the Mier prisoners—by appealing to the British to intercede on their behalf—and continued to seek an end to hostilities with Mexico that would bring freedom to all captive Texans. He succeeded to the point of signing an armistice on June 15, 1843, ending all fighting, but further negotiations failed to produce a satisfactory treaty. A few of the Mier prisoners were released from time to time at the request of the United States or foreign governments, and Santa Anna finally freed the remaining survivors in September 1844.

Houston faced numerous other problems while the Mier disaster unfolded. The most embarrassing was to some extent a difficulty of his own making—the location of the capital. He had sought to compromise with westerners who favored Austin by moving the government from Houston to Washington-on-the-Brazos, but many members of the Seventh Congress showed their displeasure by not showing up until December 1842 for a session called to meet in October. Undeterred, Houston sent a "confidential" force to Austin to bring the republic's archives back to Washington. The president's men loaded the papers on December 30, 1842, and were preparing to leave when Angelina Eberly, the manager of the Bullock Hotel, sounded an alarm and rushed out on Congress Avenue, where a small cannon was kept loaded in the event of an Indian attack. She fired it in the general direction of the government buildings, doing some minor damage to the General Land Office, and a party of Austinites left in pursuit of the archives. The chase was slow, since the papers were in three ox-drawn wagons and the pursuers were pulling their cannon with them. On the morning of the thirty-first, however, the men from Austin surrounded the camp of their quarry and forced a surrender. Both parties returned to Austin for a New Year's Eve party. Lamar's city kept the archives, but Houston would not return there so long as he was president. He had a typically practical argument: Austin's location exposed it to attack. Nevertheless, the "Archives War" and the whole matter of relocating the capital made him seem petty and selfish.

The Texas navy also became a bothersome problem. Commodore Edwin Moore finally obeyed the recall order issued by the new president shortly after his inauguration and came home to Galveston in May 1842. Securing a promise from Houston that Congress would provide funds for refurbishing the navy, Moore then took four ships to New Orleans (the other two were unseaworthy and remained in Galveston) and began repairs. That summer, Congress authorized spending $100,000 to support the navy, but Houston—as strongly committed to financial retrenchment as opposed to military adventures—only gave Moore the power to borrow money to meet his expenses in New Orleans. No financier was willing to extend credit to the Republic of Texas, so Moore's navy was in effect stranded. The commodore sought a solution by sending the *San Antonio* to Yucatán to negotiate a new agreement with federalist rebels there, but it was lost at sea. In January 1843, Houston convinced Congress to sell the navy as an unnecessary expense. Moore finally headed back to Galveston but changed his mind en route and decided to take his remaining three ships to Yucatán to help the rebels against Santa Anna's central government, which led Houston to issue a proclamation calling the commodore a pirate. Although the Texas ships fought and won several engagements with Mexican vessels, their efforts were pointless without support at home. In July 1843 the navy returned to Galveston—where Houston had Moore discharged from the service and sold the two remaining ships that had any value. Houston's policy toward the navy did not cause as much of a furor as did his refusal to invade Mexico; nevertheless, it led to additional public criticism and contributed to the resignation of his trusted friend, George Hockley, as secretary of war and marine.

Finally, 1842 also marked the outbreak of serious civil disorder in an area of East Texas centering on Shelby County. Trouble began in 1839 when Charles W. Jackson decided to expose the land commissioners of Shelby County for issuing fraudulent land titles. Jackson had been an unsuccessful candidate for Congress and blamed the commissioners and their friends for his defeat. Soon, Joseph Goodbread, a land speculator, argued with Jackson over the sale of a slave for an invalid land certificate, and Jackson killed Goodbread. The murderer and his friends then prevented a trial by the threat of violence and formed an organization called the "Regulators," supposedly to maintain order and prevent fraud. An opposing group, styling themselves the "Moderators," appeared, and the two sides began a struggle that bordered on open warfare by 1842. Houston had no armed force to handle the situation and knew that a call for volunteers would likely attract men who would take sides in the contest, so he contented himself until late in his administration with appeals to local law enforcement officials to do their jobs and for law-abiding citizens to help. Eventually, in 1844, he stationed a company of volunteers in Shelby County and brought the lawlessness to an end.

Houston's December 1843 annual message to Congress offered a positive view of the republic's affairs since he had returned to the presidency. For evidence, he pointed to the armistice with Mexico and friendly relations with the major powers, especially Great Britain; to the reduction of Indian hostilities; and to stability in public finance. In reality, however, as Houston well knew, the republic remained so insecure as to call its whole future into doubt. Currency no longer flowed from the presses, but it still circulated at depreciated rates. Moreover, in spite of all retrenchment efforts, the republic had not been able to resume paying its public debt, which would soon be more than $10 million. To add to these financial woes, bad weather had ruined the 1843 cotton crop. Foreign relations were in no better shape. The armistice with Mexico had ended hostilities for the moment, but Mexican recognition of the republic's independence was highly unlikely. Since San Jacinto, Texas had done nothing to impress any nation with its military prowess, having been unable twice to defend San Antonio against Mexican forces. Some observers wondered if it was just a matter of time until Mexico mounted a full-scale invasion and reconquered the lost province.

President Houston, ever mindful of practical realities, knew that the republic had not built the internal strength necessary to survive as a fully independent nation. Thinly populated, almost totally agricultural, financially unstable, and without a dependable military force, Texas apparently faced the alternative of submitting in some way to Mexico or turning to a major power for support. Houston would never again accept any degree of Mexican rule. Even as he spoke optimistically of Texas's progress, he was discussing the future of the republic with representatives of the governments in Washington, London, and Paris. The result was vital to the rise of the southwestern United States and to the remaining years of Houston's life.

CHAPTER EIGHT

"Annexation to the Mother Country Is Assured"

❖
❖

On January 24, 1843, Houston wrote Charles Elliot—England's chargé d'affaires in Galveston—a friendly letter in which he commented that nine-tenths of Texans who talked with him favored annexation to the United States as a means of gaining peace and security from Mexico. Leaders in Washington, regardless of their sectional loyalties, also favored annexation, he told Elliot, and both parties would advocate the policy in upcoming elections. To prevent annexation, however, it would only be necessary for Great Britain to say to Santa Anna: "Sir, Mexico must recognize the independence of Texas." The Mexican leader would welcome an opportunity to be rid of the Texas question, and—Houston implied—the republic would remain happily independent.

Houston knew that Texas had much less support in the United States than he indicated to Elliot. Northern Whigs and abolitionists screamed so loudly in rage at the mention of Texas—"All who sympathize with that pseudo-Republic hate liberty and would dethrone God," wrote William Lloyd Garrison—that those like President John Tyler who favored annexation hesitated to open the subject. Therefore, having spoken of American "interest" in Texas to spur the British, Houston next used British "ambitions" to stir the government in Washington. On January 30, 1843, Washington D. Miller, a close personal friend and advisor of the president, wrote to Tyler, expressing alarm over the success of Captain Elliot in building British influence in Texas. Most Texans, including President Houston, favored annexation, Miller wrote, but the British might overcome that sentiment by forcing Mexico to recognize the republic's independence. He urged Tyler to seize the opportunity at hand, concluding: "Let it be done before peace with Mexico is obtained. That is important." The words were Miller's, but the policy behind them was Houston's.

The Tyler administration did not respond positively to this prodding; indeed, in April, Secretary of State Daniel Webster told Texas's minister to Washington, Isaac Van Zandt, that the republic's unsettled affairs made it impossible to act. Houston, furious, poured his anger into a letter to Captain Elliot on May 13. The United States thinks that Texas is merely its "appendage," he wrote, and refuses to recognize that "we now form two nations." Once, he told Elliot, the only question facing the United States was: shall Texas be annexed? Now, he continued, "there are two: First, Is Texas *willing* to be annexed: Second, in that case, shall it be annexed?" He concluded by reiterating his belief that recognition by Mexico would lead Texas to remain independent and at least as friendly with Britain as with the United States. Elliot forwarded Houston's letter to London, where undoubtedly it proved encouraging, especially since British representatives in Mexico were helping to arrange an armistice between that nation and Texas. Houston announced the armistice on June 15 in a proclamation that recognized Britain's role in bringing peace. Some of his enemies in Texas said that he had sold out Texas to England, and the New Orleans *Picayune* accused him of agreeing to end slavery in the republic as a price for aid from London. Such charges seem to have been just what Houston wanted leaders in Washington to read.

It was not especially difficult to prompt John Tyler, a Virginian and former Democrat, to support annexation. He had succeeded to the presidency on the death of William Henry Harrison in 1841 and had quickly broken with the Whig party over issues such as rechartering a bank of the United States. The Texas question offered a president without a party an opportunity to gain favor with Democrats and Southerners and perhaps rebuild his political fortunes. When Daniel Webster—the Whig secretary of state from the antislavery stronghold of Massachusetts—resigned in May 1843, Tyler replaced him with Abel P. Upshur of Virginia. By the end of that summer, Texas's diplomats in Washington became the recipients of positive inquiries concerning annexation.

In October 1843, Upshur approached Van Zandt about a treaty of annexation, assuring the Texan that President Tyler stood ready to support it strongly. Van Zandt relayed this offer to Houston, who delayed for a while and then sent word to Upshur that such negotiations would be dangerous to Texas. Britain would drop her support, he feared, and Mexico would not sign a treaty granting independence. He did not want to risk these consequences unless the Tyler administration could assure protection for Texas in the event of a Mexican attack while negotiations were underway and guarantee passage of the completed treaty by the United States Senate. Tyler and Upshur could give no full guarantees. However, the president planned to send United States naval vessels on a "friendly" cruise in the Gulf of Mexico.

Houston remained coy through the closing months of 1843, probably with the intention of improving his negotiating position, but the Texas Congress, meeting in December, threatened to force his hand when nine-tenths of its members signed a memorial advocating immediate annexation. He responded on January 20, 1844, by sending Congress a secret message that explained his policy to that date. An unsuccessful effort by Texas to win annexation, he pointed out, would cost the republic support from Britain and France. "Hence," he argued, "the utmost caution and secrecy on our part as to the true motives of our policy should be carefully observed." Even if annexation fails, he continued, the United States might offer to negotiate a defensive alliance with Texas. Houston concluded by reminding Congress that Texas had to watch and wait for action by the United States. "If we evince too much anxiety," he said, "it will be regarded as importunity, and the voice of supplication seldom commands, in such cases, great respect."

Houston did not want to appear anxious, but he wanted Van

Zandt ready to open negotiations if success seemed likely. He began a letter of instructions on January 29 but was interrupted and did not complete it until mid-February, by which time James Pinckney Henderson had been appointed to join Van Zandt in Washington. In the first part of this letter, Houston warned Van Zandt to carry on discussions in "the most profound secrecy" to avoid alienating other nations if annexation failed. The United States, he said, "must be satisfied that all the noise about British influence has had no foundation in truth—at the same time they must be convinced that England *has* rendered important service to Texas by her mediatorial influence with Mexico." By February 15, when he completed the letter, Houston felt more confident of annexation and therefore more willing to risk alienating Britain. Glowing with optimism, he described for Van Zandt the consequences of the annexation negotiations: "Millions will realize their benefits; but it is not within the compass of mortal expression to estimate the advantages to mankind."

Houston's efforts to spur annexation by playing on the dislike of England in the United States had succeeded. "All things really prove now the *very great* desire of the U.S. to annex us," Henderson wrote Thomas Jefferson Rusk in mid-February 1844. "You would be amused to see their jealousy of England. Houston has played it off well & that is the secret of success if we do succeed." In fact, Houston had played the game so well that even Andrew Jackson had misunderstood his purpose. Old Hickory wrote several times in January 1844 to express concern over his friend's pro-British leanings. Houston's reply on February 16, which he knew would be given wide circulation, reflected his growing optimism but also carried a note of caution. "So far as I am concerned," he wrote, "I am determined upon immediate annexation to the United States." He went on to argue that in many ways the step would be more advantageous to the United States than to Texas and closed with a warning: "Now, my venerated friend, you will perceive that Texas is presented to the United States, as a bride adorned for her espousal. But if, now so confident of the union, she should be rejected, her mortification would be indescribable."

Annexation negotiations suffered a temporary setback on February 28, 1844, when Secretary of State Upshur died in the explosion of a new gun being demonstrated on the USS *Princeton*. However, President Tyler soon appointed John C. Calhoun to replace Upshur and continue the effort to bring Texas into the Union. Houston's old (and future) enemy completed negotiations with Van Zandt and Henderson, gave assurances that Texas would be protected from attack by Mexico, and signed a treaty of annexation on April 12, 1844. By its terms, Texas would become a territory of the United States. The government in Washington would acquire the public lands and property of Texas, but it would also assume the republic's public debt up to $10 million. The United States and Mexico would settle the southwestern boundary of Texas.

When Houston received a copy of the treaty on April 28, he expressed satisfaction with the terms but concern that the guarantees of Texas's security extended only to the period of negotiations. If annexation failed, the republic would be left without protection from an angry Mexican nation. Soon, developments in the United States showed that Houston had good reason for the pessimism that usually crept into even his most hopeful letters. As expected, the treaty of annexation drew bitter opposition from abolitionists and antislavery spokesmen such as Congressman John Quincy Adams of Massachusetts. Secretary of State Calhoun's letter to the British minister, Richard Packenham, explaining that annexation was necessary to protect slavery in Texas only made matters worse. The treaty's chances for approval were destroyed, however, when it became an issue in the presidential election. The probable major party nominees, Henry Clay (Whig) and Martin Van Buren (Democrat) both came out on April 27 with statements opposing immediate annexation on the grounds that it would mean war with Mexico. Apparently Clay and Van Buren had agreed in advance that this stance would remove Texas as an issue, placate antislavery opinion, and avoid problems with Mexico. Their strategy worked well for Clay, who received the Whig nomination in early May, but the Democratic party rejected Van Buren and nominated James K. Polk of Tennessee on a strongly expansionist platform. This development made the annexation of Texas a campaign issue and cost the treaty the support of many Southern Whigs, who otherwise would have voted for the addition of a new slave state. On June 8, 1844, the United States Senate defeated the annexation treaty by a vote of 35 to 16, with 15 Southern Whigs voting against Texas.

Texans reacted bitterly, but Houston did not substantially alter his annexation policy. He announced publicly that the republic was "free from all involvements and pledges" and should pursue its own national interests. And he again approached the British and French concerning guarantees of Texas's independence. However, his public announcement also said that in the event of a new offer from the United States that was unequivocal in character and removed all impediments to annexation, "it might be well for Texas to accept the invitation." As usual, he sought to keep all options open as long as possible.

Houston had little time left to negotiate because his second term was to end on December 2, 1844, and the constitution prohibited successive terms for the president. He called a general election for September 2 and watched, once again, as pro- and anti-Houston political divisions came into play. Some speculated that Lamar would run again, but the former president and others who disliked Houston supported Vice President Edward Burleson. The other candidate was Secretary of State Anson Jones. Houston made no public statement on the campaign until August 5, when in a public letter, he asserted that Jones had "concurred in my policy" and as president would promote the "honor and prosperity" of Texas. He damned Burleson with faint praise by saying that in spite of their many differences he regarded the vice president as a patriot who simply had come under the influence of selfish men. Burleson's friends then attacked Jones for being nothing more than Houston's puppet. One wit pointed out that whereas Caligula had made his horse a consul in Rome, Houston was making a "less noble animal" president. In return, Jones's friends did their best to associate Burleson with all of Lamar's discredited policies. Amidst all the mudslinging, annexation was barely mentioned. In any case, the election resulted in an easy victory for Jones. "'Old Sam,' wrote James Morgan, "can beat the D——l himself when he trys, and make anyone President."

Before Houston left office, James K. Polk, the expansionist Democrat, won the presidential election in the United States.

President Tyler, who had continued to work toward annexation even after the defeat of the treaty in June, took Polk's victory as a mandate to add Texas to the Union. He sent Congress a message in December 1844, recommending annexation by a joint resolution that would offer essentially the same terms as the treaty but would require only majority approval in both houses. Houston had already indicated, in a farewell address to the Texas Congress earlier that month, that he thought the door still open. He warned against "begging" for admission, several times advised Texas to "maintain her position firmly as it is," and spoke glowingly of the republic's future as an independent nation. However, he also said: "If the United States shall open the door, and ask her to come into her great family of States, you will then have other conductors, better than myself, to lead you into the beloved land from which we have sprung—the land of the broad stripes and bright stars." A few days later, the now ex-president prepared a memorandum setting forth the terms on which Texas would accept annexation. These included such matters as having the United States assume the republic's public debt or else allow it to keep its public lands. Houston's proposals were marked "confidential," but apparently he gave a copy to Andrew Jackson Donelson, Old Hickory's nephew, who had recently been appointed chargé d'affaires to Texas by Tyler, who in turn sent it to Secretary of State Calhoun with the recommendation that the terms be included in any annexation plan. Even out of office, Houston continued to influence the move to join Texas and the United States.

Resuming life as a private citizen, Houston planned to develop a plantation at Raven Hill, some fifteen miles from Huntsville in Walker County. Meanwhile he lived with William Bledsoe, Margaret's brother-in-law, at Grand Cane on the Trinity. Family life with Margaret and Sam, Jr., who had been born on May 25, 1843, promised a kind of happiness he had never known. It will be a joy, he wrote President Jones on December 21, 1844, to live "where the current flows in domestic peace and quiet, without one care about the affairs of Government."

In the meantime, the United States Congress, encouraged by President Tyler's annual message, began to consider proposals for bringing Texas into the Union. The House of Representatives passed an annexation resolution in late January by a vote of 120 to 98, and following minor amendments, the Senate concurred on the night of February 27 in a narrow vote of 27 to 25. The joint resolution called for Texas to enter the Union as a state rather than a territory. It would differ from all other states by retaining its public lands and its public debt. The United States would settle all boundary disputes, and new states, to a total of four, could be created from Texas with its approval. President Tyler sent the resolution to Texas on March 3, 1845, urging acceptance without reservations by the January 1, 1846, deadline set by Congress.

Houston had limited enthusiasm for the offer from Washington. He felt that the resolution amounted to dictation rather than negotiation and in many respects was unfair to Texas. For example, all public buildings, weapons, and military establishments belonging to the republic were to be turned over to the United States without any recognition that the costs of those properties had contributed heavily to Texas's public debt. Suggesting that this and other objectionable points needed to be negotiated, Houston asked Donelson to consider delaying the January 1, 1846, deadline for acceptance by Texas. While the ex-president expressed reservations, President Jones agreed to a proposal by representatives of Britain and France that their nations make one last attempt to convince Mexico to recognize Texas's independence. Jones promised to delay annexation for 90 days, thus providing time for this final effort to keep his republic from joining the United States. Houston had nothing to do with Jones's diplomatic efforts. However, since he was identified with the idea of gaining independence through British and French influence and did not immediately endorse acceptance of the offer from the United States, his enemies branded him an opponent of annexation. Because Texans overwhelmingly favored joining the Union, this charge, although fundamentally untrue, threatened his position and had to be answered. It was time for the ex-president to give a public explanation of the policy he had pursued for the past two years.

Houston planned to take Margaret and Sam, Jr., to visit her relatives in Alabama and Andrew Jackson at Nashville during the summer of 1845. On the way to Galveston in mid-May, he stopped at Houston and accepted an invitation to speak at the local Methodist church. Following a review of the San Jacinto Campaign, Houston asked the crowd's permission to answer the charges that he had been "unfaithful to the interests of Texas." He admitted that he had withdrawn the earliest request for annexation and that he had recommended treaties with England, "squinting even at the future extinction of slavery in Texas." But, he insisted, his only object had been to turn opinion in the United States in favor of annexation. Just as a woman with two suitors might use coquetry to prompt the interest of the one she favored, he said, "you must excuse me for using the same means to annex Texas to Uncle Sam." The crowd laughed and applauded, obviously in agreement with Houston's promise that "our annexation to the mother country is assured." A few weeks later, when the Houstons stopped in New Orleans on their way east, Sam made another speech, offering essentially the same explanation of his annexation policy.

Houston's enemies raged that he had lied to curry favor with the public. However, Houston's every statement indicated support for annexation if the terms were fair and the chances were good that Texas would not be embarrassed by rejection. Once again, he had pursued an objective cautiously, while keeping open as many options as possible.

Houston's pleasure at the approach of annexation was tempered by the death of Andrew Jackson on June 8, 1845. When word came to New Orleans that Old Hickory was near death, the Houston family rushed to the Hermitage but arrived a few hours too late. After the funeral, they were guests at the Donelson plantation for several weeks. Then, Houston, Margaret, and Sam, Jr., paid an extended visit to her family in Alabama and did not return home until October.

In the meantime, Texas accepted the offer of annexation. News of the congressional joint resolution had spread across the republic during the spring, touching off a spontaneous outpouring of support for joining the United States. Residents of virtually every county held mass meetings to endorse annexation. President Jones, who was playing for time to see if the British and French could convince Mexico to guarantee independence, responded to public pressure by calling a special session of the Texas Congress to meet on June 16 and a convention to meet in Austin on July 4 to consider propositions concerning the "nationality of the republic." In late May, British diplomats brought a promise from Mexico that rejection of annexation would bring a treaty recognizing the independence of Texas. Jones hoped to use this Mexican promise to convince Congress that there was time to negotiate more favorable terms with the United States. However, the Texas Senate unanimously rejected the proposal from Mexico, and both houses of the legislature unanimously accepted the annexation resolution of the U.S. Congress.

The convention met in Austin (thus returning the capital to Lamar's city, where it remained) on July 4 and immediately adopted an ordinance approving annexation. It then proceeded to write a state constitution patterned on that of the other Southern states and including protection for slavery. On October 13, 1845, Texans approved annexation by a 4,254 to 267 vote and the constitution by a vote of 4,174 to 312. The United States Congress approved the state constitution in December, and President James K. Polk signed the Texas Admission Act on December 29, 1845. All that remained was to establish a state government to take the place of that of the republic.

Houston had been elected a member of the constitutional convention from Montgomery County, but he was away in Tennessee and Alabama and did not attend. Arriving at home in October, he found his enemies still in full cry against his supposed opposition to annexation. He responded in a public letter, saying that anyone who examined his record could see that he needed no vindication. A majority of Texans agreed, because as soon as attention turned to the first elections to be held under the new constitution, he became a leading candidate for the United States Senate. "Gen. Houston's popularity in this country is undiminished," wrote Ashbel Smith in November 1845. "You may rely on his being elected one of the Senators of Texas in the next Congress."

Texans went to the polls on December 15 and elected a governor (James Pinckney Henderson), other executive officials, and a state legislature. On February 19, 1846, members of the state's new government met with the leaders of the republic in front of the capitol in Austin for a ceremony marking the completion of annexation. Anson Jones delivered his last oration as president, concluding: "The final act in this great drama is now performed. The Republic of Texas is no more." As the flag of the republic was lowered, Sam Houston stepped forward from the crowd and caught it in his arms. The stars and stripes rose in its place, and the United States took another giant stride to the southwest.

Two days after this ceremony, the Texas legislature elected Sam Houston and Thomas Jefferson Rusk to the United States Senate. Leaving Margaret, who was expecting their second child, at Raven Hill, Houston went to Galveston, across the Gulf to New Orleans, thence up the Mississippi and Ohio rivers to Pittsburgh, and from there to Washington by train. He arrived on March 28 and the next day made his first official call in the capital, a visit to James K. Polk. The president found him thoroughly Democratic and fully determined to support the administration. On the thirtieth, Rusk, who had arrived in Washington earlier, presented Houston to the Senate, and the two drew lots to determine the lengths of their terms in conformity with the constitutional requirement that one-third of the senators either retire or stand for reelection every two years. Houston drew a two-year term, which had begun with the opening of the current session of Congress in December 1845 and would end on March 3, 1847.

When the Texas senators took their seats, the Oregon country posed the most important question facing the Polk administration. In 1818, the United States and Great Britain had agreed to a joint occupation of the area from the crest of the Rocky Mountains to the Pacific Ocean between the 42nd parallel and the line 54°40'. The United States always stood ready to divide the region at the 49th parallel, a boundary already established from the Lake of the Woods to the Rocky Mountains, but the British insisted that the Columbia River serve as the dividing line. Polk, in his expansionist platform in 1844, promised the "reoccupation of Oregon," implying the whole territory north to 54°40', but after winning the election, he offered to compromise at the 49th parallel. The British, however, rejected this proposal, and Polk reacted by asking

Congress for authority to give the one-year notice terminating joint occupancy. This request drew strong opposition in the Senate from John C. Calhoun, who opposed the addition of more free territory, and from Daniel Webster, who said Oregon was not worth the risk of a war with Britain.

Houston listened to the debate for nearly two weeks and then, on April 15, 1846, broke the Senate tradition against newcomers giving major speeches. He spoke at considerable length, making numerous references to the annexation of Texas and other matters tangential to the Oregon issue, but always coming back to the defense of President Polk. The proposed end to joint occupation, he said, was necessary because delay would not bring a solution or vindicate the rights of the United States. War was not desirable, he said, but sometimes it became necessary. His vote in favor of allowing Polk to end joint occupation, he concluded, will prove "that I have not sought to embarrass the Executive, or failed to strengthen his hands while toiling for the honor, the interests, and the glory of his country." Congress soon gave Polk the authority requested, and the British, who never intended to fight over extreme claims in Oregon anyway, offered to draw the boundary at the 49th parallel. Polk put this offer into the form of a treaty, which the Senate easily approved on June 18. Houston had played no major role in the controversy, but he had the satisfaction of having backed the president in a policy that gained everything that the United States could reasonably expect. His constituents in Texas approved.

Actually, Houston and his fellow Texans gave little thought to Oregon during the late spring of 1846 because relations with Mexico were approaching a crisis. In early 1845 the Mexican minister had been called home in protest against the annexation resolution. Late that year President Polk appointed John Slidell as a special minister to Mexico with the job of reopening normal diplomatic communication and negotiating a purchase treaty that would give the United States a boundary on the Rio Grande, New Mexico, and enough of California to include the harbor at San Francisco. In the meantime, U.S. troops under General Zachary Taylor remained at Corpus Christi and did not enter the area beyond the Nueces River that Mexico denied was part of Texas.

Slidell's mission failed, however, and Polk reacted by ordering Taylor to move to the Rio Grande. On April 24, nearly a month after Taylor reached a point opposite Matamoros, a Mexican cavalry force crossed the river and clashed with a squadron of U.S. dragoons, killing 16 and capturing the rest. Polk received word of this action on May 9 and two days later, after conferring with Houston and others, told Congress that war existed by act of Mexico. The House of Representatives agreed immediately, but in the Senate, Calhoun delayed action on the grounds that a precedent might be set for allowing the president to maneuver the nation into war without a congressional declaration. Houston argued on May 11 and again on May 12 that "the state of things required prompt action—not discussion." Mexico had continued its war with Texas for ten years, he said, and after annexation had simply transferred that conflict to the United States. On May 13, the Senate passed by a 40 to 2 vote a war bill appropriating $10 million and authorizing the creation of a 50,000-man army.

There was talk back home of Houston himself leading Texas troops into Mexico. He wrote to Margaret about going "out with the army" and received her reluctant approval, but he was 53 years old and had suffered enough military hardship. Instead of leaving for the army, Senator Houston remained in Washington, working primarily in support of the war effort, until the conclusion of the first session of the Twenty-ninth Congress on August 10, 1846. He left for Texas the next day and probably arrived at Raven Hill in time for the birth of his second child, Nancy Elizabeth, on September 6.

Houston spent the fall of 1846 in East Texas, making a few appearances and speeches, but for the most part simply looking after personal affairs. He returned to Washington for the second session of Congress in December and found that, in spite of one victory after another for United States troops over Mexican forces, some senators continued to criticize the war. It was "Polk's War," they said, being fought over territory that did not belong to the United States. To make matters worse, at least from Houston's point of view, Congressman David Wilmot of Pennsylvania had injected slavery into the debate over the war. During discussion of a war appropriations bill in August 1846, Wilmot had offered an amendment providing that the South's Peculiar Institution be prohibited in any territory that might be taken from Mexico. Many Northerners, who disagreed with radical abolitionism and any hint of racial equality, supported this Wilmot Proviso because it promised only to stop the spread of slavery. It would not free the slaves, certainly not immediately, and would protect free men moving west from having to compete with black labor. For their part, most Southerners reacted angrily to the implicit condemnation of slavery by Wilmot, and hotheads soon raised the specter of secession. The House of Representatives, where the larger population of the free states gave them a numerical advantage, passed the proviso, but the Senate, due to the nearly equal number of free and slave states, did not.

On February 19, 1847, Houston spoke at length on both the criticism of the war and the slavery issue. Polk had not brought on the war, he said; Mexico had, as a result of annexation. Turning to the question of which nation had the better claim to the area between the Nueces and Rio Grande, Houston argued that the Republic of Texas had always considered the latter as its boundary and that the United States had promised to uphold that claim. In concluding, he commented on slavery, a subject soon to assume overwhelming significance in his career. He called the institution a "calamity under which the nation labored," but one that could be controlled without such extremes as disunion. Then, as reported in the *Congressional Globe*, he revealed the emotional base supporting his attitude toward slavery: "Disunion here? He could not bear the word. Let not the name of Texas, his home, the last to be incorporated into the Union, ever be blasphemed by the word 'disunion.' Let not the Union be severed. The boon we possess is too rich, too mighty, and too grand—the sum of human happiness we enjoy is too great, the amount of liberty is too precious! This question was not raised for our good. Why, was not the North dependent on the South? And was not the South dependent on the North? Would it not be to each a suicidal act? and to both destruction? Disunion! It was a monster; and if he could, he would seize upon its mane, drag it forth, and inspect its scales, and if it had a penetrable spot, he would strike it to the vitals.

"He relied upon the intelligence of the country to avoid that agitating question. He would postpone it. It was an evil which ought not to be invited; but when it shall come, let it be managed with the judgment of reasonable men, and not by passionate excitement."

Sam Houston had grown up with the Peculiar Institution and had owned slaves nearly all his life. He did not see slavery as a critical moral issue, and the "judgment of reasonable men" probably would have left blacks in bondage for generations to come. Viewed from a moral standpoint, then, his position did him little credit. On the other hand, he consistently opposed proslavery enthusiasts and insisted on preserving the Union even at the expense of limiting slavery's "rights," especially the right to expand.

Houston left Washington in March 1847, a little before Congress adjourned, because Margaret had been operated on for breast cancer. Dr. Ashbel Smith performed the surgery, and she recovered completely. That summer, believing that his family should not live so far from town, Houston traded Raven Hill for land within a few miles of Huntsville and planned to build a new home. He remained in Texas for the rest of the year, keeping abreast of the war news as General Winfield Scott's army took Mexico City in September and doing a little informal campaigning for reelection. Houston's enemies in the Texas legislature had managed to delay filling his seat when it became vacant in March, hoping that someone else might gain the position. However, on December 18, 1847, some weeks after the Thirtieth Congress had assembled, the legislature reelected Houston without significant opposition.

The most important issue on Houston's mind as he prepared to leave for Washington and a new six-year Senate term was the peace settlement with Mexico. Important Whigs such as Daniel Webster were arguing that the United States should take no territory as a result of its victory. Houston thought this position simply another way of laying blame on the United States for the war. He entered the Senate in late January 1848 and, during the next month, went on a speaking tour of New England and New York to answer the anti-expansionists. His speech in New York, although not specific as to exactly what he wanted the United

States to take from Mexico, played on all the keys of Manifest Destiny as he pictured taking control of the entire southwestern portion of North America—and maybe more—from its Hispanic owners. As sure as tomorrow's sunrise, he said, "so certain, it appears to my mind, must the Anglo-Saxon race pervade the whole southern extremity of this vast continent, and the people whom God has placed here in this land, spread, prevail, and pervade throughout the whole rich empire of this great hemisphere." From the moment your ancestors landed at Plymouth Rock, he continued, they began "cheating" the Indians out of their lands. "Now, the Mexicans are no better than Indians, and I see no reason why we should not go on in the same course now, and take their land." Houston could not resist tweaking his audience about treatment of the Indians, even as he expressed crude ethnic prejudices himself.

The senator from Texas was not pleased when the Treaty of Guadalupe-Hidalgo, signed on February 2, 1848, reached Washington. By its terms, the United States gained the Rio Grande boundary of Texas and the territory encompassing all or parts of New Mexico, Arizona, Utah, Colorado, Wyoming, Nevada, and California in return for $15 million and the assumption of debts owed by Mexico to citizens of the United States. Houston believed that the treaty did not take enough territory from Mexico but saw no likelihood of success in pursuing the matter, especially since some senators opposed taking any territory at all. On March 10, 1848, he voted to ratify the treaty. At least the war had vindicated the boundary claims that he had always made and virtually eliminated any organized Mexican threat to Texas.

As the election of 1848 approached, Houston found himself busier as a campaigner than as a senator. He made speeches in New England and New York during March and in May visited North Carolina before attending the Democratic National Convention in Baltimore. His speech to the convention defended the Mexican War and argued, somewhat cryptically, that the Wilmot Proviso "would wear itself out if left alone." Undoubtedly, he wanted both Northerners and Southerners to leave the question alone, but listeners could interpret his remark according to their sectional interests. The Democrats nominated Lewis Cass of

Michigan for the presidency, and their platform took no clear stand on the spread of slavery.

Senator John C. Calhoun, however, had no intention of leaving slavery alone. When the Senate began consideration of a bill to organize the Oregon Territory, Houston's old nemesis and other like-minded Southerners objected to the prohibition of slavery there. During the debate, Calhoun asked Houston if the bill would permit Southerners "the enjoyment of their property [slaves] as in the States where they now reside." Houston replied that the answer lay with the courts, but went on to say: "I have no idea that slavery will ever be extended to that portion of the United States; nor have I any idea that any person from the South . . . would desire to emigrate with his slaves to a region inclement as that is, and incompatible as it is with the labor." He would be the last man to do anything prejudicial to the interests of the South, he told Calhoun, but he opposed agitating the slave question when it was pointless. The bill passed by a vote of 29 to 25, and Calhoun went home angrily blaming his defeat on two Southern senators, Houston and Thomas Hart Benton of Missouri. Houston's sensible approach, intended to reduce excitement over the spread of slavery and preserve the Union, would soon become yet another weapon for his enemies in Texas.

Congress adjourned in August 1848, giving Houston an opportunity for a short visit at home, where Margaret had borne their third child, Margaret Lea Houston, on April 13 of that year. He was in Texas for the presidential election in which Texas, true to its Democratic heritage, voted for Cass. However, Zachary Taylor won the office and inherited the increasingly threatening sectional dispute over slavery.

Calhoun's determination to assert as a matter of principle the "right" of Southerners to take slave property into all the territories of the United States appeared again soon after Congress reassembled. In January 1849, he called a caucus of Southern legislators and led them in preparing an address to their constituents, charging that the North, after monopolizing all the territories, would take control of the nation and end slavery. Therefore, the South had to unite in defense of its interests. If unity did not protect Southern rights, it concluded in a thinly veiled reference to secession, then another course would have to be taken. Southern Whigs would have nothing to do with this Southern Address, but 46 Democrats signed it. Houston and Rusk refused. "You know," Houston wrote a friend in Texas, "that I am as unionfier as General Jackson was. . . ." We Texans were the last to come into the Union, he said, and "we will be the last to get out of it."

The Thirtieth Congress adjourned in March 1849, having consumed much of its time in bitter and unfruitful debate over the issue of slavery in the new territory taken from Mexico. On Texas Independence Day, Houston issued an address to his constituents explaining his position on the Oregon Territory and the Southern Address. He questioned Calhoun's authority to act as "guardian of the whole South" and accused the South Carolinian of deliberately creating Union-threatening agitation with his "abstract resolutions for extending slavery everywhere." After voicing opposition to "mad fanaticism" in the North and "mad ambition" in the South, Houston concluded with Andrew Jackson's famed 1830 response to Calhoun's theory of nullification: "The Federal Union, it must be preserved."

While Houston was home in Texas from March until November 1849, the issue of slavery in the Mexican Cession developed into a dangerous crisis. President Zachary Taylor, following his inauguration in March, attempted a simple solution to the problem by advising the residents of California and New Mexico to hold conventions, write constitutions, and apply for admission to the Union. This would bypass the territorial stage in moving from newly acquired lands to statehood, and therefore Congress would not have to decide on slavery in the territories. Since slaveholders had not taken their special kind of property into California or New Mexico, both states obviously would become free, upsetting the balance of slaveholding and nonslaveholding states and giving the North an advantage in the Senate as well as in the House. Taylor's proposals outraged Calhoun and his followers, who vowed to break up the Union rather than accept such a victory for antislavery. At the same time, to make matters worse for Houston, an issue arose concerning the western boundary of his own state. Texas, using the Rio Grande as a western limit, claimed half of New Mexico and a strip of land reaching north into

Colorado and Wyoming. Citizens of Santa Fe, the main town in that very thinly settled region, insisted that the Rio Grande was the boundary only to El Paso and that the rest of the Texas–New Mexico border was well to the east of the river. This question had obvious importance for Texas's future and sectional implications as well, because Texas was a slaveholding state and New Mexico likely would be free.

When the Thirty-first Congress assembled in December 1849, with Houston in attendance, sectional animosities were so great that it took 19 days to agree on a Speaker of the House of Representatives. President Taylor's recommendation that California—which had completed a free state constitution—be admitted to the Union led to a flurry of conflicting proposals concerning slavery in the territories. Then, on January 29, 1850, Henry Clay offered a series of resolutions intended to end the crisis through compromise. The senator from Kentucky proposed that California be admitted to the Union as a free state and that the remainder of the Mexican Cession be organized as two territories, New Mexico and Utah, without mention of slavery. The western boundary of Texas would follow the Rio Grande to the 32nd parallel, then turn directly east to the 103rd meridian, and then go due north to the line 36°30'. In return for accepting this limit on its western claims, Texas would have the United States pay its public debt. Clay also proposed compromising two other sectional disputes by outlawing the slave trade but not slavery in the District of Columbia and by passing a stronger fugitive slave law.

On February 5, Clay began what would become a six-month-long debate. Disunion would mean civil war, he said, a disaster that he hoped never to see. Three days later, Houston delivered a lengthy speech in support of compromise. Speaking before galleries so crowded that women were allowed to enter and find seats on the floor of the Senate, he advocated extending the Missouri Compromise line as the best solution to the slavery expansion issue. Territories and states north of that line would be free, and those south of it could choose slavery if they wished. Beyond this, Congress could not legislate on slavery in the states or territories of the United States. Houston criticized both the Wilmot Proviso and the Southern Address, picturing each as examples of the fanaticism that threatened the nation, and made an emotional appeal for "those whose piety will permit them" to pray for the Union. Anticipating Abraham Lincoln's famed biblical reference by eight years, Houston concluded: "For a nation divided against itself cannot stand. I wish, if this Union must be dissolved, that its ruins may be the monument of my grave, and the graves of my family. I wish no epitath to be written to tell that I survive the ruin of this glorious Union."

The speech earned much favorable comment in the Northeast, but pro-Southern Texans considered it a betrayal of their section. Houston's onetime ally, James Pinckney Henderson, condemned him for "the *damndest* outrage yet committed upon Texas." Texans had an unexpected opportunity to let their senator know how they felt, because one week after his speech he suddenly left for home. His reasons were personal—Margaret was pregnant again and had a sprained ankle, the house slaves had to be disciplined, and his overseer had left—but the newspapers imagined all sorts of explanations for his absence. When questioned about his view of the issues being debated in Washington, Houston gave no answer or joked that nothing could be done while he was absent. He had used this tactic before in time of crisis, most notably during the revolution.

Houston returned to the Senate on April 23, having been so anxious to get back that he left home just before the birth of his third daughter, Mary Willie, on April 9, 1850. As the debate continued through the spring and summer, he concentrated increasingly on the Texas boundary bill. He faced the difficult task of defending Texas's claims to the Rio Grande boundary and objecting to any unilateral attempt by the United States to settle the matter and, at the same time, avoiding any position that would endanger the compromise. Gradually, as the summer wore on, moderate opinion became stronger in the South, and by the end of September all of Clay's resolutions passed essentially as written. Houston's efforts had contributed significantly to the Texas and New Mexico Act that gave the Lone Star State $10 million as compensation for dropping its claim to territory in New Mexico, a claim that was highly questionable from the beginning. Lone Star State extremists damned the "Texas Bribery Bill," but voters overwhelmingly accepted it in November 1850. Houston not only survived the crisis of 1850 but also came home that fall a victor with an enhanced national reputation. "Old Sam," wrote Texas Congressman David Kaufman, "is on rapidly rising ground." In less than ten years, Houston had led his republic into the Union and become a successful national political leader as well.

CHAPTER NINE

"Stir Not Up Agitation!"

❖
❖

The Compromise of 1850 proved so popular that a spirit of goodwill generally pervaded the short session of the Thirty-first Congress that assembled in December. Houston enjoyed the relaxation of tensions and opposed any efforts to stir sectional feelings anew. When James Hamilton, a South Carolinian who had migrated to Texas, proposed a convention of the slaveholding states at Richmond as a first step toward seeking new guarantees of Southern rights, Houston reacted with a letter to his kinsman, Congressman John Letcher of Virginia. The Old Dominion, he wrote, should not be involved in something so unnecessary and calculated only "to protract agitation, and furnish a sort of safety valve for the overcharged patriots of South Carolina and Mississippi to let off their *extra gas*." His purpose in writing this letter, he concluded, was to stimulate Letcher and other Virginians to rescue their state from any suspicion that it would lead such a movement. Nothing came of Hamilton's proposal.

During January and February 1851, Houston lectured in Pennsylvania and New York, speaking on topics ranging from life on the frontier to temperance, but almost always managing to bring in some Texas history and a plea for the Union. When the session ended in March, he returned to Texas for a quiet spring and summer. He did some farming and apparently became so content by May that he considered retiring from the Senate. At that time, he claimed to be unwilling to serve more than part of the next session of Congress. In the early fall, however, he began making speeches in defense of his record and on December 9, 1851, took his seat in the Thirty-second Congress. A trip to Hartford, Connecticut, to speak on North American Indians, with a stop in New York to be inducted into Tammany Hall, marked the end of the year. Then he went home in February to look after business and see his newest child and fourth daughter, Antoinette Power, born on January 20, 1852.

Houston was free of serious political problems in Texas that spring. All was quiet in Washington, too, after he returned to Congress in April and spent the spring and summer serving out a very routine session. Houston enjoyed the decrease in sectional tension, but he probably regretted the calm in his personal political life because it meant that the Democratic party had passed him over in its search for a presidential nominee. He received the necessary endorsement in Texas in January 1852 when the Democratic State Convention adopted a resolution presenting his name to the national party as a candidate "eminently worthy to be the standard bearer of the party in the approaching canvass for the Presidency." However, when the Democratic convention assembled in June, he received only 8 votes to 116 for Lewis Cass on the first ballot and never gained support from more than 14 delegates. After 49 roll-call votes, the Democrats nominated Franklin Pierce, a relatively unknown senator from New Hampshire, to oppose Winfield Scott, the Whigs' military hero candidate. Pierce was identified as a friend of the Compromise of 1850, whereas Scott's platform, influenced heavily by antislavery Whigs, indicated only lukewarm acceptance.

Houston had not actively sought the nomination in 1852. Indeed, had he mounted a serious challenge, many Southern Democrats would have strongly opposed him. In any case, he missed the best opportunity that he would ever have to win the presidency. Pierce won a landslide victory over Scott, indicating public support for the compromise. Houston, as a Democrat and Southern champion of the Union, would likely have won just as easily. His role in the election, however, was limited to making a few speeches for Pierce.

While Houston was in Washington for the uneventful short session of the Thirty-second Congress from December 1852 until

March 1853, the Texas legislature, on January 15, elected him to a new six-year term in the Senate. There was opposition—3 of 22 state senators and 12 of 67 representatives voted against him—but considering the stands he had taken, his strength was impressive. All talk of retirement ended, as he looked forward to supporting such key projects as a railroad from Texas to the Pacific Ocean.

In October 1853, the Houston family moved again, this time from Huntsville to Independence, a town about 50 miles to the southwest, which attracted Houston because its schools, especially Baylor University, were reputed to be the best in the state. He paid $4,000 for a house and 350 acres of land but kept his place at Huntsville by renting it out. He also still owned a house at Cedar Point on Galveston Bay and occasionally visited there during the summer.

Houston's second full term in the Senate began in December 1853, and within a few months, the sectional calm that he had worked so hard to promote was shattered beyond repair. Senator Stephen A. Douglas of Illinois, chairman of the Senate Committee on Territories, was the chief architect of the measure that unintentionally destroyed the spirit of compromise that had prevailed since 1850. Seeking to encourage building of the first transcontinental railroad through the central United States with the eastern terminus in his state, Douglas went to work in December 1853 on a proposal for establishing territorial government in the remainder of the Louisiana Purchase west and northwest of Missouri. This would allow advocates of a central route for the railroad to argue that it would run through organized territory. The Nebraska bill, as it was originally introduced, said nothing about slavery, but under pressure from Southern Democrats who saw an opportunity to make a point if not actually spread slavery, Douglas agreed to three significant amendments. There would be two territories, Kansas and Nebraska, rather than one; the first territorial legislature elected in each would decide whether or not to have slavery; and the Missouri Compromise restriction on slavery north of 36°30' would be repealed. In other words, the Kansas-Nebraska Act, as it became known, would apply the concept of "popular sovereignty" and let the voters of each territory decide slavery's fate. The repeal of the Missouri Compromise restriction gave proslavery forces an opportunity to take the Peculiar Institution into territory closed to them for 34 years. Douglas knew that the act would raise, as he put it, "one hell of a storm" in the North, but he badly wanted the territory organized and convinced himself that the storm would blow over without lasting damage, especially since slavery had little value in the region.

The Kansas-Nebraska bill went to the Senate on January 23, 1854, and debate began a week later. Antislavery senators angrily attacked the author as well as the bill, and Douglas repaid all personal attacks in kind. Since Democrats controlled both houses of Congress, passage of the bill was almost certain. Nevertheless, Houston let it be known that he intended to stand against his party and his section and vote in the negative. A foretaste of the South's reaction came from a correspondent of the Richmond *Enquirer*: "Nothing can justify this treachery; nor can anything save the traitor from the deep damnation which such treason may merit."

Houston's speech explaining and defending his opposition to the Kansas-Nebraska bill took most of two days, February 14 and 15, 1854. He devoted the first day entirely to a defense of the Indians who were to be removed from millions of acres of land as a necessary step in opening the new territories. He concluded: "A Redeemer was given to the world, but the Indians have as yet found no Saviour. They have no salvation to look to but in the justice of this Government. Is it not time that justice, tardy justice, be done?" These remarks were hardly calculated to make Houston popular anywhere in the United States, but the next day would be even worse where the South was concerned. On the fifteenth, he condemned the repeal of the Missouri Compromise, pointing out that it represented a compact between the sections that his own party often had pledged to support. Moreover, he said, the compromise, as a practical matter, protected the South— the minority section—far more than the North. Repeal it, he said, and the free-soil majority will soon overwhelm the slaveholding interest. Repeal was shortsighted and potentially destructive. He did not wish to be regarded as for the South alone, he continued. But, his identity was there, his life had been spent there, and it was his duty to stand up in behalf of her rights and to secure every guarantee for her safety and her security. The choice was between harmony and prosperity or anarchy and civil conflict.

The Senate agreed to vote on the bill on March 3, but the debate continued past midnight, and Houston gained the floor for a final speech in the early morning hours of the fourth. He went over again all the arguments in favor of maintaining the Missouri Compromise and answered those who insisted that the issue was one of principle, that slavery had to have the right to go into all territories. Insistence on such a principle, he said, will be "fatal to the future harmony and well-being of the country." Nearing the end of his speech, Houston asked the Senate what Henry Clay and Daniel Webster, champions of the Compromise of 1850 who had left their country in peace, would think of this effort to undo all their work. He raised his voice in a final plea—*"Maintain the Missouri Compromise! Stir not up agitation! Give us peace!"*—and prophesied that union or disunion depended upon the decision about to be made. Just before five in the morning, the voting began, and the Kansas-Nebraska Act passed by a vote of 37 to 14. Houston and John Bell of Tennessee were the only Southerners voting with the minority. The House passed the bill 113 to 100 on May 22, but by then the tumult had begun.

Free-soil spokesmen across the North attacked the Kansas-Nebraska Act in sermons, speeches, and newspaper editorials, and the public became agitated as never before over the expansion of slavery. Douglas remarked that he could walk from Boston to Chicago by the light of burning effigies of himself. Ironically, since he had opposed Douglas's act, Houston received a similar, if not quite so "warm," welcome when he returned to Texas in April 1854. He came home because Margaret was enduring a difficult pregnancy (her sixth child, Andrew Jackson Houston, would be born on June 21), but rumor had it that he had come to resign from the Senate. Longtime political enemies, joined by secessionists and proslavery enthusiasts, enjoyed the opportunity to attack Houston as a traitor to the South. More distressingly, many old friends turned their heads and would not speak when he approached. Houston tried to make Texans see that "the most unpopular vote" he ever gave was also "the wisest and most patriotic." He told them, as he had said in the Senate, that the Missouri Compromise protected the South and that repeal would invite political retaliation from the more powerful North. Forces unleashed by the Kansas-Nebraska Act, he prophesied, would result by 1860 in the election of a free-soil president. Secession and war would follow, and the South will "go down in the unequal contest, in a sea of blood and smoking ruin."

Houston remained in Texas until June, discussing the situation with those who remained his friends and making several speeches to polite but unresponsive audiences. When he returned to the Senate, no one could judge exactly how much support his vote had cost him at home. He had survived generally unacceptable policies such as defending the Indians, refusing to attack Mexico, and negotiating with the British; perhaps personal popularity would sustain him again.

Washington was relatively quiet during the summer of 1854 as the immediate furor over Kansas-Nebraska died down and the act's more serious consequences remained in the future. Houston made several speeches in response to criticisms of his handling of the Texas navy and the Mier Expedition when he had been president of Texas, but he did not have to debate sectional issues in the Senate. Returning to Texas in October, he completed the reformation of his personal life by being baptized into the Baptist Church. Dr. Rufus C. Burleson performed the ceremony at Rocky Creek near Independence on November 19, 1854.

The summer of 1854 marked the emergence of a new political party. In July, nativists, who regarded immigrants and Roman Catholics as dangerous to the United States, formed the American party and pledged never to vote for any foreign-born or Catholic candidate for office. Because they were instructed to answer all questions about the movement with the words "I know nothing," their organization became known as the Know-Nothing party. Houston, although at times critical of Catholic Mexico, had never exhibited strong nativist tendencies, but soon he became identified with the Know-Nothings. In January 1855, he responded to an allusion to his supposed interest in the new party by saying to fellow senators: "Now, of the Know-Nothings I know nothing; and of them I care nothing." He admitted supporting some of their principles, especially the restriction of immigration to people of good character, but his remarks did not constitute a strong commitment to Know-Nothingism. Nevertheless, rumors flew, and Texas Democrats had yet another reason to oppose Sam Houston.

Those who attacked Houston as a traitor to the South never seemed to notice that he did not speak for or against slavery as such, but only refused to fight for the principle that it had a right to enter all the territories of the United States. In February 1855, he broke his customary silence on the merits of the institution itself by accepting an invitation to speak on the subject at Tremont Temple in Boston. The audience was certain to be filled with abolitionists, especially since William Lloyd Garrison was to reply; so it provided the sort of challenge that Houston relished. He pointed out that slavery had existed in all the American colonies and had become associated with the South alone at the time of the Revolution. The institution lived on in the South because of the need for labor; it died in the North because immigrants provided wage laborers. Southerners, he argued, used slaves but treated them well in every respect. The South depended on their labor, but so did the mills of the North. Moreover, there was the problem of what the slaves would do if they were freed. They could not take care of themselves and would be worse off than as bondsmen. All the South asked, he said, was to be let alone to control its own domestic institutions. Turning to the issue of slavery in the territories, Houston once more argued for acceptance of the Missouri Compromise line. He concluded by begging for an end to misunderstanding between the sections. "Our country is too glorious, to[o] magnificent, to[o] sublime in its future prospects, to permit domestic jars or political opinions to produce a wreck of this mighty vessel of State."

Houston, like the great majority of his white contemporaries North and South, did not see slavery as a moral evil to be eradicated at all costs, and he allowed racism to stand in the way of seriously considering emancipation. However, he defended slavery as a practical necessity and stopped well short of the more aggressive view associated with John C. Calhoun and other extremists that the institution was a "positive good." Houston's moderate views on slavery provided one more basis for his unionism throughout the antebellum years.

Houston came home in March 1855 for his first extended stay since passage of the Kansas-Nebraska Act. During that spring and summer, he made speech after speech, defending his record and expressing confidence that the people of Texas would support him as they always had. His enemies, he told a crowd at San Jacinto in July, "may fester in the putrescence of their own malignity. They cannot hurt or disturb me." Unfortunately for Houston, however, state elections, scheduled for August 1855, allowed his enemies to make an issue of his Know-Nothingism as well as his votes on slavery expansion.

The Democratic party held its state convention on April 21 but made no nominations, recommending only that the incumbents, Governor E. M. Pease and Lieutenant Governor David C. Dickson, be continued in office. Then, on June 11, Know-Nothing party leaders nominated Dickson as their gubernatorial candidate, forcing the Democrats to call a "Bomb Shell" convention in Austin and replace Dickson with Hardin R. Runnels as their candidate for lieutenant governor. Asked for his views on the Know-Nothings as the election approached, Houston published an open letter that endorsed the movement and sought to link it with unionism. He supported excluding immigrants who could not obtain certificates of good character from consuls and insisted that the American movement was "not to put down the Catholics, but to prevent Catholics putting down Protestants." The letter emphasized unionism rather than nativism, reminding Texans that Democrats had passed the Kansas-Nebraska Act, aroused the abolitionists, and ruined the sectional calm after the Compromise of 1850. Does the "*modern* Democracy," he asked, stand on the Jackson or Calhoun platform? "Jackson's was the Constitution and the Union," he said, and that is where I stand. Houston's letter did not help the Know-Nothings on election day. Although Lemuel D. Evans won a seat in Congress, Dickson and most of the party's other candidates lost to their Democratic opponents.

Having disposed of the Know-Nothing challenge, the Democrats went into full cry after Houston during the ensuing months before the state legislature met in November 1855. Mass meetings in county after county passed resolutions denouncing his vote against Kansas-Nebraska and his support of the American party. Gonzales County Democrats, for example, concluded "that the interest of the slave State of Texas is not safe at this crisis in his hands." Newspaper editors echoed this sentiment, asking the legislature to express its lack of confidence in Senator Houston.

Houston arrived in Austin before the legislature met and on November 23 attended a barbecue given by the Know-Nothings in his honor. He spoke at considerable length, reviewing his entire senatorial career and elaborating his now-favorite argument that the Democratic party had been taken over by supporters of Calhoun, whereas he still stood for the party of Jackson. I have but two planks in my platform, he said, "*the Constitution and the Union.* By the one I am guided, with the other I am willing to perish." Three days later Texas's state senators and representatives passed by a vote of 77 to 3 the following resolution: "that the Legislature approves the course of Thomas J. Rusk in voting for the Kansas-Nebraska Act and disapproves the course of Sam Houston in voting against it." Although his term had a little more than three years remaining, this resolution showed Houston that only a dramatic turn of events could save his Senate career. Most Texans still respected his past services, but at that point they would not accept his refusal to vote for slavery's right to expand.

After Houston left for Washington and the Thirty-fourth Congress in December, the outcry against him continued in Texas. Several newspapers called for his resignation, and the Democratic State Convention, meeting in January 1856, passed a resolution condemning his Kansas-Nebraska vote as not in accord with "the sentiments of the Democracy of Texas." The Know-Nothing party, meeting a week later, said nothing in defense of Houston. Know-Nothingism in Texas was already on the decline, dooming Houston's hope that it could become a vehicle for unionism. Indeed, Know-Nothing nativism had strengthened his opponents by driving normally unionist Germans into the Democratic party.

Houston arrived in Washington in January 1856 to find Congress with its attention fixed on developments resulting from the Kansas-Nebraska Act. Elections for the first territorial legislature of Kansas, held in March 1855, had been marked by pro-slavery residents of Missouri crossing into the new territory to vote. The resulting legislature drafted a slave code for Kansas, but free-soil settlers refused to accept laws based on fraud and set up a rival government. During the spring of 1856, violence erupted as a proslavery "posse" raided Lawrence to arrest free soilers who opposed the slave code, and John Brown subsequently led a party of antislavery men to murder and mutilate five Southerners on Pottawatomie Creek. Events in "Bleeding Kansas" led to angry debate and even to violence in Washington. In May 1856, Senator Charles Sumner of Massachusetts delivered a speech on Kansas that attacked several senators, especially Stephen A. Douglas of Illinois and Andrew P. Butler of South Carolina, in extremely personal terms. Congressman Preston Brooks of South Carolina took revenge a few days later by approaching Sumner while he worked at his desk in the Senate and beating him severely with a stout cane.

Houston took no part in the debates over Kansas, focusing instead on largely routine matters, and he was home in Texas, visiting his family and recuperating from a bronchial infection, during the Sumner-Brooks episode in May. Undoubtedly the agitation and violence disturbed him, but from his point of view, another result of the Kansas-Nebraska Act was even more threatening. The measure had split the Whig party and led to its replacement in the North by the Republican party. Although the new party was controlled not by abolitionists but by free soilers who only opposed the spread of slavery, most Southerners failed to appreciate the distinction. Democrats across the South began to threaten secession the moment any "Black Republican" candidate won the presidency. Houston's prophetic fears about the impact of Kansas-Nebraska had begun to come true.

The campaign for the presidency in 1856 turned into a three-way race as the Democrats nominated James Buchanan; the Know-Nothings, Millard Fillmore; and the Republicans, John C. Frémont. Houston looked over the field during the late summer and found himself unenthusiastic about any of the candidates. The Democratic party, he believed, had deserted the principles of Jackson and, by repealing the Missouri Compromise and endorsing the Kansas-Nebraska Act, stirred up agitation that threatened the Union. The Republicans, with their sectional platform and principles, were equally dangerous. Under those circumstances, he supported the Know-Nothings because, he told the Senate in August, "they go for the Union out and out, or I would not act with them."

Houston also made it very clear to the Senate that, although he disagreed with the Republicans, he thought talk of secession in the event of victory by the new party "not worthy of an American." I dislike the idea of a sectional candidate, he said, but if "he receives a constitutional majority of the electoral votes, and be elected according to the Constitution, I shall recognize him as chief magistrate of my country. I will submit; every patriot will submit."

Fortunately for Houston, the results of the election of 1856 did not force him to face the question of submitting to a Republican. Texas and the other Southern states voted for Buchanan, and the Democratic candidate also carried enough Northern states to win. The badly beaten Know-Nothing party soon disappeared, but Houston, whose support had been lukewarm at best throughout the campaign, apparently had no regrets. He went back to Washington for an uneventful short session of Congress from December 1856 to March 1857 and returned home in the spring, seemingly torn between two options—retiring from public life or continuing to fight for the Union and for vindication by the people of Texas.

On May 12, 1857, Houston announced as a candidate for governor of Texas in the election scheduled for August. The decision to run came after the Democratic State Convention, meeting in Waco on May 4, nominated Hardin R. Runnels, a disciple of Calhoun, and made the issue very much a matter of Houston and anti-Houston. "The people want excitement," he wrote Rusk, "and I had as well give it as anyone." As usual, Houston was true to his word. Riding in a crimson buggy furnished as a promotion by a salesman for "Warwick's Patent Plow" and often sleeping on the ground at night, he traveled throughout the state and made at least sixty speeches during a little more than sixty Texas summer days. The pace was punishing for a 64-year-old man, but the excitement carried him on. Democratic spokesmen such as Louis T. Wigfall and Williamson S. Oldham followed Houston, reminding Texans of the senator's votes on slavery expansion and calling him a traitor to the South. In reply, Houston explained his belief that Southern extremism increased threats from the North rather than protecting the South, and he launched amusing attacks on his leading critics. Wigfall was dubbed "wiggletail"; Oldham, accused of defrauding an Arkansas bank and sinking its books in the White River. John Marshall, editor of the Austin *Texas State Gazette*, Houston said, would not eat meat and "one drop of his blood would freeze a frog."

Houston's fight was all uphill. He stood on the "wrong" side of the most emotional issue in Southern history—expansion and the long-range future of slavery. The Democratic party, which had always controlled Texas politics, and its press united behind Runnels, whereas Houston was essentially a man without a party. Even old friends such as Rusk and Ashbel Smith, who did not turn against him personally, indicated that they supported his opponent. Under these circumstances, Houston's loss, by a vote of 32,552 to 28,678, was less remarkable than the relatively narrow margin of defeat. His 47 percent of the vote testified to the personal popularity of "Old San Jacinto" and, to a lesser extent, to the unionism that might still be tapped to prevent secession in Texas.

Houston took defeat well, writing to Ashbel Smith on August 22, "The fuss is over, and the sun yet shines as ever. What next?" His enemies, of course, took pleasure in pointing out that the voters had repudiated him and in calling for his resignation from the Senate. He remains in Congress, the Austin *Texas State Gazette* said, "merely to receive his *per diem allowance*." In November, the Texas legislature had to elect a senator to replace Thomas J. Rusk, who had committed suicide in July, just before the election. After selecting James Pinckney Henderson to Rusk's seat, the legislators went ahead and elected Judge John Hemphill to replace their other senator, although his term would not end for nearly two years. Houston ignored this additional pressure and went to

Washington for the opening of the Thirty-fifth Congress in December 1857.

Still indulging his flair for unusual clothing, Houston went to the Senate wearing a waistcoat made of leopard skin. A friend admired the coat and was told, "I have chosen to wear [it] . . . because the scripture says 'a leopard cannot change his spots.'" One "spot" that Houston certainly did not intend to change was his view of the Kansas-Nebraska Act, the results of which were still disturbing Congress and the nation. The proslavery territorial legislature of Kansas, elected in 1855 with the aid of residents of Missouri, had attempted to use its momentary advantage to create a new slave state. A convention, chosen in an election boycotted by distrusting free-soil settlers, met in Lecompton in 1857 and drafted a constitution that would have brought Kansas into the Union as a slave state. The territory's voters were not given an opportunity to reject the entire constitution. In late 1857, when the Lecompton Constitution reached Washington, it ran into opposition not only from Republicans but also from Senator Stephen A. Douglas and some other Democrats. Douglas sincerely believed in popular sovereignty and would not support a constitution that obviously did not represent the will of the majority of the people in Kansas.

Houston wrote Margaret that the latest problems from Kansas were "the offspring of the repeal of the Missouri Compromise" and a vindication of his position. He spoke only twice during the Senate debate on the Lecompton Constitution. First, he rose on March 19, 1858, to deny the charge by Senator Clement C. Clay of Alabama that those who had voted against the Kansas-Nebraska Act did so because it opened the territory to slavery. I opposed the measure, Houston said, not as an enemy or a friend of slavery, but because it threatened sectional peace. Almost wearily, he explained once again that he was not antislavery or anti-Southern. "I cherish every manly sentiment for the South," he said, "and I am determined that while I live in it, none of the fraternal bonds which bind it to this Union shall be broken." Then, four days later, he announced his intention to vote for the Lecompton Constitution, claiming that he was merely following instructions from the Texas legislature. Perhaps, since he had never supported popular sovereignty or been an advocate of slavery restriction, he found it relatively easy to follow instructions and swallow a fraudulent constitution, especially since the great majority of Texans favored it. This action was not characteristic of Houston, but apparently he was tired of the Kansas question and hoped to end the agitation. In any case, the Lecompton Constitution, after passing the Senate, was blocked in the House, and by a compromise agreement was sent back to Kansas for a true referendum. Given an opportunity to come into the Union immediately under the Lecompton Constitution or wait for some years, the people of the territory voted down the constitution overwhelmingly.

In mid-February 1858, while the Kansas question was pending, Houston introduced a resolution calling for investigating the possibility of establishing a United States protectorate over Mexico and Central America. His purpose, he told startled senators who accused him of advocating filibuster adventures, was not to extend "our dominion" but rather to improve "our neighborhood." Mexico and the Central American nations were so unstable, he said, that they could not control their own populations or protect themselves from other powers. The Senate refused to bring this resolution to a vote. The motive behind Houston's proposal is not clear. Perhaps he was seeking a diversion for a nation wracked with sectionalism, or he may have genuinely wanted to continue expansion to the southwest. Whatever his purpose, this resolution was no more than a trial balloon, and nothing came of it.

Regardless of his "lame duck" status, Houston did the best he could during the winter and spring of 1858 to represent Texas. For example, he continued to advocate a southern route for the proposed transcontinental railroad and recommended completing the boundary survey between Texas and New Mexico to settle land titles. However, he could do nothing that pleased Democratic leaders and editors in the Lone Star State. When Senator James Pinckney Henderson died in June, Houston eulogized him as a man of bold spirit, strong will, and firm purpose. The Austin

Texas State Gazette responded by damning Houston as a hypocrite and slanderer for praising a man whom he had attacked during the 1857 gubernatorial campaign.

As the session moved toward a close in June, Houston thought more and more about the joys of retiring to his family. He arrived home to be greeted by yet another child, William Rogers, born on May 25, 1858, and then proceeded to behave like a man far from ready to end his career and live in simple retirement. In August and September, he made at least five political speeches, defending his record and pointing to the evils that had followed passage of the Kansas-Nebraska Act. "I think," wrote an anonymous observer of one of these speeches, "there is no doubt about the fact that sober second thought is slightly mollifying the bitterness of his bitterest enemies." When Houston left in December for the short term of the Thirty-fifth Congress, some Texans expected him to return in the spring of 1859 as a candidate for governor.

Houston spoke frequently during his valedictory session in the Senate. On January 12–13, 1859, he responded to Senator Alfred Iverson of Georgia, who had injected threats of secession into a debate over the transcontinental railroad. Houston pointed, with more emphasis than before, to the many practical reasons for opposing secession. "Will they cut the great Mississippi in two?" he asked. Think of the conflict that will create. "Sir, it is madness." In February, Houston spoke at great length concerning the impeachment of John Watrous, judge of the federal district court for eastern Texas. Watrous, who was notoriously corrupt, especially in land deals, remained on the bench until 1861. Nevertheless, the speech attacking the judge won praise for Houston across Texas, even from many of those who had been bitterly critical of him. Finally, on February 28, four days before the end of the session, he spoke in response to new charges made by his enemies in Texas that he had been a coward rather than a hero during the San Jacinto Campaign in 1836. In closing, he expressed faith that the Senate would lead in securing "the perpetuity of the Union."

Houston left Washington for Texas on March 10, 1859. A local newspaper commented: "Up to the hour of his departure, his rooms were crowded by his friends calling to take leave of him.

No other public man ever made more, or more sincere[,] friends here, nor was severance of a gentleman's connection with American public affairs ever more seriously regretted than in his case." Houston never returned to Washington, but the report of his "severance" from public affairs was premature. His efforts to prevent agitation by fellow Southerners had cost him national office, but he would continue the fight in Texas.

CHAPTER TEN

"Whipsters and Demagogues"

❖
❖

Immediately upon his return to Texas in March 1859, Sam Houston took up the role of a 66-year-old man who seemingly had reached the end of his public life. He spent the early spring at Cedar Point on Galveston Bay, enjoying his family and giving every indication that he intended to pursue a quiet retirement. In the meantime, however, newspapers, especially George W. Paschal's Austin *Southern Intelligencer*, began to carry editorials and letters suggesting that the people of Texas were waking up to the wrong done to Houston and were ready to restore him to a position of leadership. He should be placed, one letter said, where he can "continue to stay the tide of *Disunion*, rebuke *Sectionalism*, war upon *Black Republicanism*, and, above all, fearlessly expose corruption in high places, as long as he lives." Proslavery extremists opposed Houston as much as ever, but as the furor over the Kansas-Nebraska Act and his flirtation with the Know-Nothing party receded into the past, the reputation of the Hero of San Jacinto reasserted its hold on many Texans. If Houston wished to remain in politics, perhaps as a candidate for governor, the situation was far more favorable than at any time since 1854. "I think the Old Dragon will run again," his brother-in-law wrote on April 1, 1859. "The reaction in his favor is wonderful."

The Democratic State Convention on May 2 increased the likelihood of a Houston candidacy by renominating Governor Hardin R. Runnels and giving serious consideration to a plank endorsing reopening the African slave trade. This proposal did not pass, but it provided additional proof of extremism among regular Democrats and new impetus to the surge in favor of the former senator. Later in May, the National Democrats, as Houston's supporters began to call themselves, rallied in Austin and adopted a resolution asking "That all freemen who are opposed to the opening of the *African Slave trade, Secession*, and other Disunion issues . . . unite with us in electing Genl. Sam Houston for Governor." Paschal, who publicized every bit of pro-Houston news that came to his attention, also appealed to Houston's friends such as Ashbel Smith to convince him to run. "The people will elect Houston," he wrote, "whether he will or not."

Houston made no response to these developments until June 3. Then he sent Paschal a brief note saying that he had "yielded my own inclinations to the inclinations of my friends" and concluded to serve as governor if elected. "The Constitution and the Union embrace the principles by which I shall be governed if elected," he wrote. "They comprehend all the old Jackson National Democracy I ever professed, or officially practised." Houston almost certainly appreciated the opportunity for vindication, but there is no evidence that he actively sought to become a candidate. Moreover, in sharp contrast to 1857, he did not campaign once he agreed to run. Texans who wanted his leadership had drawn him into the contest, and they did the campaigning. Paschal's *Southern Intelligencer* ran the headline: "The Agony Over—SAM HOUSTON IN THE FIELD," beginning a contest among pro- and anti-Houston editors, orators, and letter writers that did not end until election day on August 1, 1859.

Houston remained out of the fight except for a few public letters and a single speech. When Ferdinand Flake, editor of the German-language *Die Union* in Galveston, questioned him about Know-Nothingism, Houston replied that no such organization had existed in Texas since 1855. Rejecting all "isms," a reference undoubtedly covering the nativism that concerned Flake, the candidate insisted that the Constitution and the Union offered freedom and liberty to all men.

Houston's lone speech of the campaign came when he visited Nacogdoches on business in early July and gave in to the urgings of local citizens that he address them. He began by pointing out that he was a "Democrat of the Old School" who did not need the endorsement of a convention to prove his membership in the party. True democracy, he said, rises from the people, and it is at their request that I am a candidate. Two years ago, he told the voters, "you whipped me like a cur dog" because of my opposition to the Kansas-Nebraska Act, but now many Southerners realize that the measure was only a *"delusion and deception from the beginning."* Since 1854, he said, I have remained true to the same principles that directed my course then—a desire to avoid agitation and uphold the Constitution and laws made under it. He condemned equally Northerners such as Senator William Seward of New York who called for violating the Fugitive Slave Act and Southerners such as extremist Democrats in Texas who advocated disobedience to laws against the African slave trade. Departing from the Constitution, he warned, would bring a horrible civil war.

Turning to matters not directly associated with the key issue of union versus disunion, Houston reminded his audience that he had always supported a southern route for the transcontinental railroad and that his proposal for a protectorate over Mexico would bring stability and prosperity to that nation while protecting the interests of United States citizens. The Indians of Texas, he said, should be placed on reservations well removed from white settlements, and the frontier should be protected by rangers. Finally, he advocated a system of public education that would be as free as possible but not "extravagant."

On August 1, 1859, Houston defeated Runnels by a vote of 33,375 to 27,500, roughly the same margin by which he had lost two years earlier. Runnels had lost support due to accusations that he had not protected settlers during Indian warfare on the frontier in 1858 to 1859 and charges of extravagance in government spending. However, Houston's victory was primarily a tribute to his personal popularity and to the vitality of unionism in Texas. While he was winning the governorship, another unionist, A. J. Hamilton, running as an independent, won a seat in the United States House of Representatives. Certainly, ultra-Southerners from South Carolina to Texas saw Houston's success as a bitter defeat for their cause. The Charleston *Mercury* called him a "traitor who ought to fall never to rise again," and Runnels wrote privately that the new governor's "Demagogical Union saving doctrines" would "inflict an irreparable blow upon Southern interests at this time."

Houston remained quiet until Inauguration Day on December 21, 1859, speaking only at barbecues given in his honor at Huntsville and Montgomery in September. On both occasions, he repeated the arguments made at Nacogdoches in July, although he did make a point of exempting Runnels from criticism. Houston had no immediate comment in October when the abolitionist John Brown attacked Harpers Ferry in Virginia, but he must have shaken his head wearily with the knowledge that Northern extremism would only fan the flames of Southern extremism. Brown's raid probably influenced the state legislature's decision in November to elect the ultra-Southerner Louis T. Wigfall to the United States Senate, but he might well have been chosen anyhow. Houston's victory had not carried with it control of the Texas House and Senate by Independents, and Wigfall's election was a sign of what the new governor would face. The House blocked an appropriation to pay for new furnishings in the executive mansion and even debated allowing the use of its chamber for an inaugural ball.

Houston responded to this animosity by arranging his own inaugural festivities, including the delivery of an address from the front porch of the capitol. After taking the oath of office and becoming the only man in the United States ever to serve as governor of two different states, Houston began his speech to applause that, according to one observer, shook the capitol. He promised state aid for railroad building and river improvement and advocated "the improvement and perfection of common schools." On the subject of frontier defense, Houston returned to his favorite recommendations—the use of mounted rangers and the exertion of "moral influence" on the Indians by fair treatment. Border relations with Mexico, he said, depended on the national government, but if disorders reached from Mexico across the Rio Grande, he would take strong action to protect Texans. The new governor then pled with his listeners to remember that when Texas joined the United States, "She entered not into the North, nor into the South, but into the Union. . . ." Please distinguish, he said, between the wild ravings of fanatics and the moderation of the masses of the people and do not fall prey to sectional extremism. He pointed out that the people had elected him; therefore, he concluded, if the legislature insisted on giving attention to "national abstractions" that had no place in state government, "I have but to look to the people to sustain me." In little more than a year, events would belie Houston's optimism.

The Houston family moved into the governor's mansion, and the new chief executive began to wrestle with the state's problems. He had inherited a serious difficulty in the Brownsville area rising from conflict between Anglo-Texans and Mexicans from both sides of the Rio Grande led by Juan N. Cortina. The Anglos saw Cortina as a murderous bandit, whereas he appeared to his own people as a defender of their rights to land claims and equal justice. In the late fall of 1859, Cortina won several battles against local volunteer forces and began to fly the Mexican flag and talk of taking back all land between the Rio Grande and the Nueces. However, shortly after Houston assumed the governorship, a force of U.S. Army regulars and Texas Rangers defeated Cortina in a battle at Rio Grande City. One final skirmish with the Rangers in February 1860 ended the Cortina Wars. Governor Houston issued a proclamation in late December ordering all armed bands to disperse, but he was careful not to blame anyone for the trouble on the Rio Grande. Instead, he sent Angel Navarro III of San Antonio and Robert H. Taylor of Fannin County to determine the causes of the conflict.

The governor also acted quickly to deal with the threat of Comanche and Kiowa attacks on the frontier. He urged the United States to send cavalry to Texas and to make fair settlements with the Indians, but in the meantime he had the government of Texas take strong action, too. By the end of March 1860, he directed the creation of seven companies of frontier rangers totaling more than 500 men and also authorized the chief justice of each county to raise a company of minutemen. These state forces, with the aid of federal troops in western forts, by the end of 1860 overawed the Indians to such an extent that peace generally prevailed on the frontier.

Houston also kept a concerned eye on sectional issues. His first formal message to the legislature on January 13, 1860, concluded with comments on the seeming "triumph of conservatism" in the rejection of John Brown by a majority of Northerners, a development that he hoped would "stay the hand of slavery agitators" in the South. Within a week, however, he received a set of resolutions from the South Carolina legislature indicating that Southern extremists had no intention of resting. The resolutions, accompanied by a letter from the governor of South Carolina asking that they be submitted to the Texas legislature, asserted the right of states to secede from the Union. Houston complied with the request, but he also sent a lengthy message condemning disunion as unnecessary, impractical, and contrary to the historical development of the United States. Quotations from George Washington, Thomas Jefferson, James Madison, Andrew Jackson, Henry Clay, and Daniel Webster supported his argument. Texas, he concluded, is satisfied with the Constitution and the Union and should work to allay the "morbid and dangerous sentiment" of sectionalism.

Nothing came of the South Carolina resolutions in early 1860, but Houston, regardless of his optimistic statements, knew that the upcoming presidential election promised renewed, and more threatening, extremism. James Buchanan's lackluster administration had weakened the Democratic party in the North. Meanwhile, Southern Democrats had worked themselves into a "rule-or-ruin" mood, insisting that they would bolt unless their party's platform and candidate would support slavery's rights in all the territories. A split in the Democratic party would greatly improve the chances of victory for the Republican party, an event that many Southerners promised would lead immediately to secession.

As the campaign of 1860 approached, a few observers thought that the Democratic party might turn to Sam Houston as a candidate. His unionism made him acceptable to many in the North, and his gubernatorial victory indicated renewed popularity in Texas (and perhaps the South). On January 20, 1860, a group of unionist Democrats from Galveston wrote the governor to inquire if his name could be put into consideration at the Democratic National Convention scheduled to meet at Charleston, South Carolina, in late April. Houston's reply unequivocally rejected the Democratic party and the convention system of nomination. The party, he wrote, has been taken over by factions—"National men have given place to sectional agitators"—and no nominee of the Charleston convention will be able to appeal to the North to sustain the Constitution and the Union. "If my name should be used in connection with the Presidency," he concluded, "the movement must originate with the people themselves, . . . I will not consent to have my name submitted to any Convention."

Houston stood on principle in refusing to pursue the Democratic nomination, but his proposed candidacy had no chance on practical grounds either. The state party convention, meeting in Austin during early April, chose six Southern extremists to represent Texas at the convention in Charleston. Houston was not in step with the majority of Democrats in his state, and he could never have won the support of a delegation headed by Guy M. Bryan and including former governor Hardin R. Runnels.

Realistically, Houston's only chance of becoming a candidate in 1860 lay with conservatives of both sections, men who feared the extremism of the major parties and would unite spontaneously behind a strong leader who promised to save the Union. As early as January 1860, a mass meeting of unionists in New York nominated the Texas governor for president. Lone Star State Unionists added impetus at a meeting of what they called the "National Democracy" in Austin on March 20. Speaker after speaker extolled the virtues of Sam Houston, and the group reassembled two days later to adopt resolutions endorsing him for the presidency and establishing a committee to correspond with his supporters across the nation. A month later Houston's supporters in Texas turned the anniversary of San Jacinto into a spectacular campaign rally. Numerous old Texans listened as Isaac L. Hill of Fayette County announced that their purpose was to recommend Sam Houston for the presidency. The meeting then adopted resolutions pledging loyalty to the Union, endorsing Houston's candidacy, and urging support by "all conservative men, of all parties, in all sections of the Union."

Two days later, the Democratic Convention assembled in Charleston. Southern extremists insisted that the platform endorse federal protection for slavery in all the nation's territories and, when they failed to obtain such a plank, walked out of the meeting. The entire Texas delegation came home. Since Democratic party rules required a two-thirds majority to win the nomination, the withdrawal of the delegations from eight states meant that the convention could not name candidates. It broke up, planning to meet again in Baltimore in mid-June. In the meantime, the Republican party assembled in Chicago on May 16, 1860, and adopted a platform that rejected abolitionism but opposed the spread of slavery and shrewdly appealed to Northern economic interests. Abraham Lincoln, an antislavery moderate from Illinois, became the party's candidate. The Democrats, when they reconvened in Baltimore in June, ignored the virtual certainty that a split in their party would hand victory to the Republicans. This time upper Southerners walked out over the issue of whether to readmit delegates from the deep South who had bolted at Charleston. Those who remained nominated Stephen A. Douglas, making him in effect the candidate of the Northern Democratic party. Southern Democrats met a few days later and chose John C. Breckinridge of Kentucky as their standard-bearer.

During the spring of 1860, Sam Houston could only watch, in sorrow but not with surprise, as the party of Jackson brought the Union closer to dissolution. Totally disgusted with the Democratic party, he effectively renounced all organized political groups and claimed to have confidence only in the people of the United States. This meant that he did not involve himself in the Constitutional Union party that emerged under the leadership of border-state politicians such as the former Whig, John J. Crittenden of Kentucky. Constitutional Unionists represented exactly the views that Houston had preached throughout the sectional crisis, but he made no effort to become a leader or a candidate for the new party's nomination. Nevertheless, when the party met in convention in Baltimore on May 9, one observer reported that "there are many who are anxious to avail themselves of the battle of San Jacinto." The Texas delegation of four conservative unionists, led by the spectacularly bearded A. B. Norton who had sworn never to shave until Henry Clay became president, put Houston's name before the convention. On the first ballot, John Bell of Tennessee received 68½ votes to Houston's 57. A second ballot resulted in an increase of 12 votes for Houston, but shifts of support from other candidates moved Bell close enough to a majority that a switch of a few votes gave him the nomination. Edward Everett of Massachusetts became the vice presidential candidate.

In a public letter written a week after the Constitutional Union party convention, Houston noted that the submitting of his name there "was entirely unauthorized by me, and opposed to my well known opinions." "The people alone have the nominating power," he wrote. Exactly how "the people" were to make a nomination and their candidate was to develop a serious campaign without benefit of a convention or party organization is difficult to imagine, and it seems doubtful that Houston, who was usually practical and realistic, entertained much hope for such a development. Nevertheless, on May 17, in response to his "nomination" by the meeting at San Jacinto, he wrote: ". . . if the independent masses of the country deem my name important, in connection with the Presidency, they have a right to use it." One week later, he informed the editors of the Clarksville *Standard* that "I have responded to the people of San Jacinto, and have consented to let my name go before the country as the People's Candidate for the Presidency."

Houston attracted some support across the country during the late spring and early summer of 1860, especially in New York where a mass meeting on May 29 sang his praises and declared for the Constitution and the Union. The "People's Candidate," however, never became a significant factor in the national contest and only added to the confusion of Texas unionists. Bell was their candidate, but they preferred Houston, and to make matters worse, projects for uniting Bell, Douglas, and even Breckinridge supporters swirled around the state. By mid-August, Sam Houston saw that Southerners, whether unionists or extremists, were going to lose the election. He could never vote for Lincoln, he told a friend, and would vote for Douglas, Bell, or Breckinridge only to save the Union. He could not see, however, how the withdrawal of any two of those candidates could bring victory to the third. "What would it avail," he asked, "if I should come out and cry Huzaa for Breckinridge, when if he were to get the vote of the United South it would not elect him?"

Houston recognized that his own candidacy had failed. "Nothing but the wisdom of Devine Providence," he wrote, "can so dispose matters as to advance the wishes of my friends." Accordingly, on August 18, he issued a statement withdrawing his name from the list of presidential aspirants. He did not endorse any candidate, but made it clear that above all he opposed a Republican victory. Once more, as he had on so many occasions, Houston called on Americans to remember the words of Andrew Jackson: "The Federal Union, it must be preserved."

On August 12, Houston's personal life was brightened by the birth of a son, Temple Lea, the last of eight children borne by Margaret Lea Houston. Nothing, however, could ease for long the pressure of building sectional tensions. On September 22, he left his sick bed to speak at length to a Union mass meeting in Austin. What rights have we lost? he asked the audience. Our property has not been taken from us, and all constitutional guarantees are in place. Of course, we wish to see the Republicans defeated, he continued, but Lincoln's election would give "no excuse for dissolving the Union. The Union is worth more than Mr. Lincoln. . . . If Mr. Lincoln administers the Government in accordance with the Constitution, our rights must be respected. If he does not, the Constitution has provided a remedy." He closed by damning the "whipsters and demagogues" who sought to mislead the people and pleading that the "calamitous curse of disunion" not be visited upon future generations of Texans. His audience cheered, but popular reaction, fueled by extremist newspapers such as the Marshall *Texas Republican* and Dallas *Herald*, was largely negative.

As the election neared, Houston stepped up his efforts against disunion, making numerous speeches in the central Texas region from Austin to Huntsville during late October. His Thanksgiving Day Proclamation, issued on October 27, asked Texans to pray that God would "shield us still in the time of peril, that we may be preserved a United people, free, independent, and prosperous." He spent election day, November 6, 1860, in Austin and the next day, although not knowing for certain that Lincoln had won the presidency, confided his worst fears in a letter to Sam Houston, Jr. "The price of liberty is blood," he wrote his eldest son, "and if an attempt is made to destroy our Union, or violate our Constitution, there will be blood shed to maintain them. The Demons of anarchy must be put down and destroyed. The miserable Demagogues & Traitors of the land, must be silenced, and set at naught." The governor was preparing mentally for his last battle.

The secession movement in Texas began immediately upon arrival of the news that Lincoln had been elected president. In towns all across the state, public meetings passed resolutions vowing no submission to the "Black Republicans" and calling for a convention to consider disunion. Leaders of the government in Austin, including Supreme Court Justice Oran M. Roberts, Attorney General George M. Flournoy, and John S. "Rip" Ford, met to discuss methods of making secession a legal and orderly process. The disunionists, however, faced one huge obstacle. Only the state legislature, which was not scheduled to meet until the next year, had the legal authority to call a convention, and only the governor could call the legislature into special session. Once again, extremism ran into Sam Houston's hardheaded unionism.

The governor and his supporters hoped that delay would have a calming effect on the mania for secession. To this end, Houston urged Texans to wait and see if Lincoln would violate the Constitution. "So long as the Constitution is maintained by the 'Federal authority,'" he wrote on November 20 to a group of Texans who asked his opinion on the crisis, "and Texas is not made the victim of 'federal wrong' I am for the Union as it is." "Passion is rash," he reminded them, "wisdom considers well her way." Houston also played for time by dusting off a joint resolution passed by the state legislature in February 1858 calling for a meeting of representatives of the Southern states to consult on means of preserving their equal rights. A convention, he told other Southern governors on November 28, "may result in the adoption of such measures as will restore harmony between the two sections of the Union." Five days later, as a capstone to his delaying tactics, Houston addressed the people of Texas with the message that no action could or should be taken until the other Southern states responded.

Secessionists refused to be deterred by the governor's opposition. On December 3, prominent leaders of the movement met in Attorney General Flournoy's office and issued a call for a convention to be elected on January 8, 1861, and assemble in Austin on January 28. The urgency of the situation, they argued— "the insults, threats and aggressions" from the North—justified action without approval of the governor or legislature. Houston responded with a testing of the political waters in Galveston and his namesake city on December 7 and 8. His speech in the Queen City evoked cheers from an originally hostile crowd, but in Houston he was interrupted by cheers for William Yancey, Alabama's secessionist hothead. Returning to Austin, the governor called the legislature into special session for January 21, 1861, one week before the convention was to meet. Some interpreted this as a surrender, but anyone who remembered Houston's San Jacinto Campaign should have understood it as a strategic retreat. The special session, his proclamation indicated, was necessary to allow the "whole people" to determine the proper course for Texas "to maintain, if possible, her rights in the Union, as guaranteed by the Federal Constitution." Perhaps the legislature could be used to head off the convention.

Houston's task became more difficult on December 20 when South Carolina seceded, providing new impetus and enthusiasm for Texas disunionists. Although his cause was slipping away, he continued to pursue the idea of a convention of the Southern states to protect their rights within the Union. On December 21, he and his friends organized a "Union Club" to promote such a meeting, and on the twenty-seventh, he issued a proclamation for the election of seven Texas delegates. Secessionists denounced the Southern convention idea as, in the words of the Dallas *Herald*, a "puerile effort to mislead the people."

As the new year opened, Houston began to work on yet another fallback position intended to protect Texas from destruction in civil war. He would yield to secession, he told a crowd at Waco, if the people of Texas voted for it, but then the state should remain independent rather than joining a Southern confederacy. Texas should, he said, "unfurl again the banner of the Lone Star to the breeze and reenter upon a national career." A week later he elaborated the same view in a letter to J. M. Calhoun, Alabama's commissioner to Texas. When states secede independently without waiting for unified action, he wrote, this shows Texans that their cooperation in a Southern confederacy is not considered necessary and justifies them in avoiding "entangling alliances" and entering once more upon a "national career." If the Union is dissolved and civil war follows, he told Calhoun, at least Texas will be responsible for herself. Finally, to make his image of returning to independence more appealing, Houston argued that Texas had views of expansion not common to her sister states. "She will not be content to have the path of her destiny clogged," he wrote. "The same spirit of enterprise that founded a Republic here, will carry her institutions Southward and Westward."

On January 20, the day before the legislature met, Houston gave another indication that, although in retreat, he was by no means ready to surrender. He sent a Texas Ranger captain to warn General David E. Twiggs, commander of United States troops in Texas, of the rumor that a mob planned to take federal property, including arms and ammunition, that was under his control. The governor offered assistance in resisting the attack and suggested that Twiggs might consider putting the property in the hands of state authorities for safekeeping. If the secessionists turned to force, Houston meant to be ready.

When the special legislative session met on January 21, the governor's message examined Indian policy and financial problems at length before turning to secession. The heart of his message was an attempt to have the legislature reject the convention scheduled to meet a week later. The people of Texas, he said, alone can determine what will happen, and they should be given an opportunity to speak in a "legitimate manner." He promised not to oppose the legislature should it decide to call a "convention of delegates fresh from the people," but he recommended that no action be considered final until it had been submitted to the voters. In conclusion, Houston asked the legislature to reject those who want to "plunge madly into revolution." "The Executive has not yet lost the hope," he said, "that our rights can be maintained in the Union, and that it may yet be perpetuated." A letter from Margaret Houston to her mother, written that same day, revealed the strain behind this legislative message. "General Houston seems cheerful and hopeful through the day," his wife wrote, "but in the still watches of the night I hear him agonizing in prayer for our distracted country."

The legislature acted immediately to support the secession movement. It repealed the 1858 resolution that Houston had used as a basis for recommending a convention of the Southern states and then approved the convention scheduled to meet on the twenty-eighth. That meeting, the legislators said, properly represented the will of the people of Texas. Houston's wishes were followed only in one particular—any action taken by the convention had to be ratified in a popular referendum.

The secession convention assembled on January 28 and the following day by a vote of 152 to 6 passed a resolution approving secession by Texas. This killed the last hope of adopting Houston's plan for a Southern convention and left only the formality of adopting an ordinance of secession. After two days of debate on the wording of that statement, the final vote came on February 1. Houston, seeing that the convention overwhelmingly favored disunion, could only hope that somehow the people, whose voice he promised to obey, would save Texas or that at least the state would not join the Confederacy. Perhaps these hopes persuaded him to accept an invitation to be present at the convention on the first and give symbolic approval to secession. Seated beside the presiding officer, Judge Oran M. Roberts, the governor watched in silence as the convention approved destruction of his beloved Union by a vote of 166 to 8. As the cheering ended and Houston rose to leave, Roberts remarked that it was good to have him present. Houston replied without emotion, "I hope that we will have many happy days yet."

On February 9, Houston issued a proclamation calling a statewide referendum on secession for the twenty-third. Also, early that month he reminded the legislature that disunion meant a great many additional responsibilities and expenses for state government. If the legislature provides the means, he wrote, the governor will see "that the honor and interest of Texas do not suffer in his hands." The governor watched without reaction on February 18 as Ben McCulloch, acting for the convention, took control of United States property in San Antonio from General Twiggs. Some extremists sneered at what they called Houston's "conversion," but the governor in a letter made public on February 20 dared anyone to find a single word that he had spoken in favor of secession. "I have declared myself in favor of peace, of harmony, of compromise, in order to obtain a fair expression of the will of the People," he wrote. "I still believe that secession will bring ruin and civil war. Yet if the people will it, I can bear it with them."

On February 23, 1861, the voters of Texas endorsed secession by a margin of 46,153 to 14,747. News of the final tally on March 3, the day after Houston's sixty-eighth birthday, evoked cheers and the ringing of bells in Austin, but according to one of his daughters, the old man in the Governor's Mansion, his jaw set and his face ashen, said to his wife, "Texas is lost." The next day, Houston issued a proclamation announcing the secession of his state. He had only one defensive position left—to have Texas maintain its independence rather than join the Confederacy. That, he hoped, would afford some chance of avoiding civil war.

In early February, without waiting for the referendum, the secession convention had sent representatives to Montgomery, Alabama, the first capital of the Confederate States of America. Now, on March 5, the convention adopted an ordinance formally joining Texas with the new Southern nation. Houston, seeing this action as unauthorized by the legislature or by the people, challenged it head on. Once the secession question had been submitted to the people, he told the convention, its "powers were exhausted." When the Confederate secretary of war, Leroy P. Walker, informed Houston that his government had assumed control of military operations in Texas, the governor replied on March 13 that the people of his state would never be annexed without their knowledge or consent.

Determined to destroy Houston's last defense, the convention voted on March 14 to require all state officials to take an oath of loyalty to the Confederacy. The governor did not appear on the fifteenth, so that night George W. Chilton presented him with an order that he appear at noon the next day. Nancy Houston, the family's oldest daughter, remembered vividly the events that followed at the Executive Mansion. After dinner, Houston read from the family Bible and retired to an upstairs bedroom, removing his shoes so that his pacing would not disturb his wife and children. He came down, said to his wife, "Margaret, I will never do it," and returned to spend the rest of the night writing an address to the people of Texas, explaining his refusal. Before noon, he went to the capitol but not to his office or to the lobby. Instead, he sat in the basement, whittling a piece of soft pine. Three times the secretary of the convention called his name—"Sam Houston! Sam Houston! Sam Houston!"—but he sat without moving except to continue whittling.

The convention declared the governor's office vacant and on March 18 elevated Lieutenant Governor Edward Clark to the position. In the meantime, Houston issued the address he had begun on the night of the fifteenth. Its argument was simple—everything that the convention had done since submitting secession to a popular referendum was usurpation of power. He would not attempt to hold his office by force, he said, because he did not wish to bring strife and bloodshed upon Texas. If he could no longer hold the governorship peacefully, he would withdraw, although still claiming to be the chief executive. When the legislature assembled on March 18, Houston sent them essentially the same message, reviewing the record of the secession crisis and decrying the illegal actions of the convention. He pointed out again that he had the power to call out the militia but had not because he believed that "the calamities of civil war would be greater than the endurance of this usurpation for a time." The message concluded with a plea to restore Texas to its rightful government and a promise that, if driven to retirement, he would remain loyal to his state.

Houston rejected suggestions that he attempt to hold the governorship by force. On March 19, as he and his family packed under orders from the convention to leave by the twentieth, messengers arrived with word that a group of his friends were armed and ready to put him back in office. Houston reacted in horror at the thought of anyone "willing to deluge the capital of Texas with the blood of Texans, merely to keep one poor old man in a position for a few days longer, in a position that belongs to the people." More than likely Houston would have received only limited military support from Texans, but he responded in the same fashion to offers that could have put significant force at his disposal. Twice during March and April—the precise dates are unknown—Abraham Lincoln offered Houston military aid in holding Texas for the Union. "Had I been disposed to involve Texas in civil war," the deposed governor wrote later that year, "I had it in my power, for I was tendered the aid of seventy thousand men [doubtless an exaggerated number] and means to sustain myself in Texas by adhering to the Union; but this I rejected. . . ." The flag of the Confederacy flew over the capitol as Houston left Austin.

Houston's role in the secession crisis drew criticism from both secessionists and unionists. The former called him a "submissionist" who sought to betray the South, and many of the latter, especially outside Texas, accused him of cowardice and lack of leadership. In reality, Governor Houston was a Southerner who loved his section and state, a democrat who accepted the will of the people, a realist who favored strategic retreat when faced with overwhelming opposition, and an old man with a young family. As the secession mania mounted, he fell back slowly from one position to another but found no way to prevent disunion or joining the Confederacy. There were no offers of help until it was too late to maintain the Union without civil war in Texas. The larger war that was to come had not begun when he received Lincoln's offer; to have accepted it, regardless of the number of troops offered, would likely have made the Lone Star State the first battlefield in a conflict that he hoped never to see.

The Houston family left Austin for Cedar Point on Galveston Bay, but road conditions forced them to stop at the home of Margaret's mother in Independence for several months. Leaving his wife and children there, the ex-governor went on to Galveston in late March. En route, he visited Brenham, where old friends invited him to speak. He declined at first but changed his mind when local secessionists vowed that he would not be heard. As he rose to speak in the packed courthouse, some cried "put him out" and "kill him," but a planter named Hugh McIntyre, drawing his pistol and jumping on a table, threatened to shoot anyone who did not keep quiet. Houston told the crowd that demagogues had succeeded in "stilling the voice of reason" in Texas and that, as a result, "The soil of our beloved South will drink deep the precious blood of our sons and brethren." "The die has been cast by your secession leaders," he said, "and you must ere long reap the fearful harvest of conspiracy and revolution." His predictions would prove as accurate as they were courageous.

Houston was in Galveston on April 12, 1861, when the Confederacy fired on Fort Sumter and began the war that he so feared. Back in Independence on May 10, he told a crowd at the Baptist Church that the guns at Sumter had drowned the "voice of hope" and forced all men to choose. "The time has come," he said, "when a man's section is his country. I stand by mine." The old soldier went on to warn Texans that the war would require unity, discipline, and perseverance. Drawing upon the memories of his struggles in 1835 to 1836, he told his audience: "A good motto for a soldier is, Never underrate the strength of your enemy. The South claims superiority over them [the North] in point of fearless courage. Equal them in discipline, and there will be no danger." Houston's support for the Confederacy once the war came does not call into question the sincerity and strength of his unionism. True, he could have continued to support the United States, even to the point of becoming an exile from Texas, but that would have been too much to ask of a 68-year-old democrat whose whole life depended on the South. Sam Houston simply had to defend Texas as a parent would defend a child. He had taken every reasonable step to prevent disunion and joining the Confederacy; now, he could only stand with his state and hope for the best.

Houston's advice to his eldest son concerning military service indicated the defensive nature of his stand. Sam, Jr., having completed the spring term at Allen Military Academy, was at Cedar Point and anxious to join the army. Houston urged him not to let "anything disturb you; attend to business, and when it is proper, you shall go to war, if you really wish to do so. It is every man's duty to defend his Country; and I wish my offspring to do so at the proper time and in the proper way. We are not wanted or needed out of Texas, and we may soon be wanted and needed in Texas. Until then, my son, be content." Sam, Jr., with a fine disregard for parental wishes that Sam, Sr., should have appreciated, joined the first volunteer unit raised in the area and left for the war as a member of Company C, Second Texas Infantry. On April 7, 1862, Sam Houston, Jr., fought in the terrible battle at Shiloh, and his name appeared on the list of Southern "dead and missing." Six months later, to his parents' great joy, he appeared at Cedar Point, haggard and on crutches, but alive. He had survived a severe wound by a minié ball and had been imprisoned at Camp Douglas before being exchanged and returning to Texas. Eventually, Sam Houston, Jr., would return to the army and serve out the remainder of the war.

Houston had much to endure during the spring and summer of 1862. His son was missing in the war, and yet many in Texas still held him suspect and called him a traitor. In May, General Paul O. Hebert, commander of all Confederate troops in the state, declared martial law, a step that Houston saw as unnecessary and dictatorial. He protested angrily to Governor Francis R. Lubbock: "Acquiescence to usurpation is—SLAVERY! Is necessity urged in behalf of such things? My answer is *necessity* is the plea of *tyrants*, and the exercise of *unrestrained will* is the throne of *Despotism*!" To a friend he wrote in August 1862: "If it were the will of my Heavenly Father that I should enjoy a tranquil evening and close of life, I would be thankful—but His will be done!"

In October 1862, United States forces took Galveston, bringing the war very close to Cedar Point and destroying the Houston family's main source of income, the supply of firewood to the island city. Houston had to move again, this time to Huntsville, where he rented a house that had been built to resemble a stern-wheeler steamboat. The "Steamboat House" would be his last residence, for during the winter of 1863, his health began to fail. The old man's war wounds—especially the one to the shoulder received at Horseshoe Bend—bothered him, and he developed a persistent cough. His mind remained active, however, even as his body failed. He was delighted when General John B. Magruder recaptured Galveston on January 1, 1863, and traveled to his namesake city for a major speech on March 18. He expressed optimism that Texas and the Confederacy would yet succeed but, ever the realist, warned that the "period is approaching when the great issues of the war will be decided. The turning point must soon come." When the decisive battles came—at Gettysburg and Vicksburg in July 1863—Sam Houston lay dying of pneumonia.

On July 26, as his wife read the Bible at his bedside, Houston spoke for the last time—"Texas . . . Texas . . . Margaret."

*   *   *

Sam Houston provided leadership essential to the southwestern expansion of the United States during the first half of the nineteenth century. He, more than any other individual, assured the success of the Texas Revolution and kept the republic alive until it became part of his "mother country." Annexation of Texas led to the Mexican War, which, in turn, resulted in the acquisition of California and the rest of the American Southwest.

Houston failed to stem the rising tide of sectionalism during the 1850s and to prevent the rush to secession in 1860 to 1861. His leadership, however, displayed courage and prophetic wisdom virtually unmatched among politicians across the South. He ended his career rather than take a step that would involve his beloved state in the tragedy of the Civil War.

Sam Houston's personal shortcomings, especially his years of heavy drinking, became legendary during his lifetime, but strengths of character and mind more than compensated for his weaknesses. Houston possessed courage, not just the physical courage to lead men into battle but also the moral courage to stand for his beliefs regardless of the consequences. He had the kind of ambition and pride that leads men to excel. He liked to command, others saw him as a commander, and in leadership positions, he would never do anything unworthy. Finally, courage, pride, and ambition were tempered by practicality. Whether commanding a revolutionary army, presiding over an infant republic, or opposing secession, Houston never lost sight of practical realities. A dash to join the heroes of the Alamo in 1836, a war of revenge on Mexico in 1842, an assertion of Southern invincibility in 1860—such actions would have shown courage and pride and served ambition, but they would not have been practical. The personal key to Houston's greatest achievements lay in his good sense. What an irony for a man whose life was so filled with romantic adventure.

A Note on the Sources

The basic compilation of Houston's letters, speeches, and messages is Amelia Williams and Eugene C. Barker, eds., *The Writings of Sam Houston, 1813–1863* (8 vols., Austin: University of Texas Press, 1938–1943). This work contains more than 2,500 entries, drawn primarily from Houston's papers in the Barker Texas History Center at the University of Texas and in the Library of Congress, and approximately 10,000 explanatory footnotes. One sizable manuscript collection not available to Williams and Barker, the Andrew Jackson Houston Papers, has since been given to the Texas State Archives. Important Houston letters from 1835 to 1836 not published in the *Writings* are found in John H. Jenkins, III, ed., *The Papers of the Texas Revolution, 1835–1836* (10 vols., Austin: Presidial Press, 1973). Houston told his own story up to 1850 in *Life of General Sam Houston: A Short Autobiography* (Washington: J. T. Towers, 1852[?]; reprint, Austin: Pemberton Press, 1964). Once the author's extreme praise for himself is discounted, this autobiography offers valuable clarification of key events in Houston's life.

The writings of contemporaries are a rich source on Houston, especially during the years of the revolution and the republic. These include William Bollaert, *William Bollaert's Texas*, edited by W. Eugene Hollon and Ruth Lapham Butler (Norman: University of Oklahoma Press, 1956); William Fairfax Gray, *From Virginia to Texas, 1835: Diary of Col. Wm. F. Gray, Giving Details of his Journey to Texas and return in 1835–1836 and Second Journey to Texas in 1837*

(Houston: Gray, Dillaye & Co., 1909); John Holland Jenkins, *Recollections of Early Texas: The Memoirs of John Holland Jenkins*, edited by John Holmes Jenkins III (Austin: University of Texas Press, 1958); John Joseph Linn, *Reminiscences of Fifty Years in Texas* (New York: D. & J. Sadlier & Co., 1883); Ashbel Smith, *Reminiscences of the Texas Republic . . .* (Galveston: Historical Society of Galveston, 1876); Noah Smithwick, *The Evolution of a State: Or, Recollections of Old Texas Days*, compiled by Nanna Smithwick Donaldson (Austin: Gammel Book Company, 1900); and Adolphus Sterne, *Hurrah for Texas! The Diary of Adolphus Sterne, 1838–1851*, edited by Archie P. McDonald (Waco: Texian Press, 1969). Anti-Houston diatribes by contemporaries include Robert M. Coleman, *Houston Displayed; Or, Who Won the Battle of San Jacinto? By a Farmer in the Army* (Velasco, TX: 1837) and Thomas Jefferson Green, *Journal of the Texian Expedition against Mier . . .* (New York: Harper & Brothers, 1845). Carlos E. Castañeda, trans., *The Mexican Side of the Texas Revolution* (Dallas: P. L. Turner, 1928), presents the views of Houston's chief opponents in 1836, including Santa Anna, Tornel, and Filisola. There is even a memoir by one of Houston's slaves: Jeff Hamilton, *My Master: The Inside Story of Sam Houston and His Times*, edited by Lenoir Hunt (Dallas: Manfred, Van Nort & Co., 1940).

Several early histories of Texas contain useful material prepared by Houston's contemporaries. Henderson K. Yoakum, who wrote *History of Texas from Its First Settlement in 1685 to Its Annexation to the United States in 1846* (New York: Redfield, 1855), was a close friend of Houston's and used sources provided by Houston and other leaders such as Thomas Jefferson Rusk. Dudley G. Wooten, *A Comprehensive History of Texas, 1685–1897* (Dallas: William G. Scarff, 1898), reprinted Yoakum's history and included material written by numerous mid-nineteenth-century leaders. DeWitt Clinton Baker, *A Texas Scrap-Book, Made up of the History, Biography, and Miscellany of Texas and Its People* (New York: A. S. Barnes & Co., 1875), is another compilation of sources on early Texas history.

Houston has attracted dozens of biographers. The first was Charles Edwards Lester, who wrote what amounted to a campaign biography—*Sam Houston and His Republic* (New York:

Burgess, Stringer & Co., 1846)—shortly after Houston became a United States senator. A second version by Lester appeared during the mid-fifties, *The Life of Sam Houston (The Only Authentic Memoir of Him Ever Published)* (New York: J. C. Derby, 1855). At the request of Margaret Lea Houston, William Carey Crane wrote *Life and Select Literary Remains of Sam Houston of Texas* (Philadelphia: J. B. Lippincott, 1884). The first attempt at a scholarly biography was Alfred M. Williams, *Sam Houston and the War of Independence in Texas* (Boston: Houghton Mifflin, 1893). By far the most successful literary biography is Marquis James, *The Raven: A Biography of Sam Houston* (Indianapolis: Bobbs-Merrill, 1929), which won a Pulitzer Prize. This highly readable book captured fully the romantic flair of Houston's life, and only occasionally went beyond what can safely be documented. Llerena B. Friend, *Sam Houston: The Great Designer* (Austin: University of Texas Press, 1954), is the most scholarly biography, but it pays little attention to Houston's early years. The study with the most balanced coverage of Houston's life and well-balanced interpretations of all the controversies in which he was involved is Marion K. Wisehart, *Sam Houston: American Giant* (Washington, DC: Robert B. Luce, 1962). Two recent biographies, Donald Braider, *Solitary Star: A Biography of Sam Houston* (New York: G. P. Putnam's Sons, 1974), and Clifford Hopewell, *Sam Houston: Man of Destiny* (Austin: Eakin Press, 1987), do not measure up to those by James, Friend, and Wisehart.

Houston has been the subject of numerous specialized studies and interpretive essays. Jack Gregory and Rennard Strickland, *Sam Houston with the Cherokees, 1829–1833* (Austin: University of Texas Press, 1967), provides information on this important interlude. Sue Flanagan, *Sam Houston's Texas* (Austin: University of Texas Press, 1964), combines biographical information and photographs into an interesting presentation. Thomas H. Kreneck, "Sam Houston's Quest for Personal Harmony: An Interpretation" (Ph.D. diss., Bowling Green State University, 1981), is a psychobiography that emphasizes conflict in Houston between a desire for harmony and stability and an adventuresome desire for success. Important interpretive and special-topic articles include Joe B. Frantz, "Texas Giant of Contradictions: Sam Houston,"

American West, 17 (July/August 1980), 5–12, 61–65; Ernest C. Shearer, "Sam Houston and Religion," *Tennessee Historical Quarterly*, 20 (March 1961), 38–50; Edward R. Maher, Jr., "Sam Houston and Secession," *Southwestern Historical Quarterly*, 55 (April 1952), 448–458; and Andrew F. Muir, "Sam Houston and the Civil War," *Texana*, 6 (Fall 1968), 282-287.

Biographies of Houston's most important contemporaries, although uneven in quality, also shed light on his career. See William Seale, *Sam Houston's Wife: A Biography of Margaret Lea Houston* (Norman: University of Oklahoma Press, 1970); Eugene C. Barker, *The Life of Stephen F. Austin, Founder of Texas, 1793–1836* . . . (Nashville and Dallas: Cokesbury Press, 1925); Charles P. Roland, *Albert Sidney Johnston: Soldier of Three Republics* (Austin: University of Texas Press, 1964); Herbert P. Gambrell, *Mirabeau Buonaparte Lamar: Troubador and Crusader* (Dallas: Southwest Press, 1934); Robert G. Winchester, *James Pinckney Henderson: Texas's First Governor* (San Antonio: Naylor Company, 1971); Mary W. Clarke, *Thomas J. Rusk: Soldier, Statesman, Jurist* (Austin: Jenkins Publishing Co., 1971); Elizabeth Silverthorne, *Ashbel Smith of Texas: Pioneer, Patriot, Statesman, 1805–1886* (College Station: Texas A&M University Press, 1982); Mary W. Clarke, *David G. Burnet* (Austin: Pemberton Press, 1969); John H. Jenkins and Kenneth Kesselus, *Edward Burleson: Texas Frontier Leader* (Austin: Jenkins Publishing Co., 1990); Herbert Gambrell, *Anson Jones: The Last President of Texas* (Garden City, NY: Doubleday, 1948); Ben H. Proctor, *Not Without Honor: The Life of John H. Reagan* (Austin: University of Texas Press, 1962); and Alvy L. King, *Louis T. Wigfall: Southern Fire-Eater* (Baton Rouge: Louisiana State University Press, 1970).

Context for Houston's role in the Texas Revolution is found in Eugene C. Barker, *Mexico and Texas, 1821–1835: University of Texas Research Lectures on the Causes of the Texas Revolution* (Dallas: P. L. Turner Co., 1928); Ohland Morton, *Terán and Texas: A Chapter in Texas-Mexican Relations* (Austin: Texas State Historical Association, 1948); David J. Weber, *The Mexican Frontier, 1821–1846: The American Southwest under Mexico* (Albuquerque: University of New Mexico Press, 1982). The well-known but unsubstantiated claim that the revolution resulted from a conspiracy led by

Andrew Jackson and Houston is found in Richard R. Stenberg, "The Texas Schemes of Jackson and Houston, 1829–1836," *Southwestern Social Science Quarterly*, 15 (December 1934), 944–965. William C. Binkley, *The Texas Revolution* (Baton Rouge: Louisiana State University Press, 1952), a series of lectures, still provides the most focused overview. The fighting of the revolution is well summarized in James W. Pohl and Stephen L. Hardin, "The Military History of the Texas Revolution: An Overview," *Southwestern Historical Quarterly*, 89 (October 1985), 137–164. See also Alwyn Barr, *Texans in Revolt: The Battle for San Antonio, 1835* (Austin: University of Texas Press, 1990); and James W. Pohl, *The Battle of San Jacinto* (Austin: Texas State Historical Association, 1989).

Major works on the Republic of Texas include the following: Stanley Siegel, *A Political History of the Texas Republic* (Austin: University of Texas Press, 1956); Joseph W. Schmitz, *Texan Statecraft, 1836–1845* (San Antonio: Naylor Company, 1941); William R. Hogan, *The Texas Republic: A Social and Economic History* (Norman: University of Oklahoma Press, 1946); Joseph Milton Nance, *After San Jacinto: The Texas-Mexican Frontier, 1836–1841* (Austin: University of Texas Press, 1963); Nance, *Attack and Counter-Attack: The Texas-Mexican Frontier, 1842* (Austin: University of Texas Press, 1964); Sam W. Haynes, *Soldiers of Misfortune: The Somervell and Mier Expeditions* (Austin: University of Texas Press, 1990); and John Edward Weems, *Dream of Empire: A Human History of the Republic of Texas, 1836–1846* (New York: Simon & Schuster, 1971). Thomas Lloyd Miller, *The Public Lands of Texas, 1519–1970* (Norman: University of Oklahoma Press, 1972); Edmund T. Miller, *A Financial History of Texas* (Austin: Bulletin of the University of Texas No. 37, 1916); Walter Prescott Webb, *The Texas Rangers; A Century of Frontier Defense* (Boston: Houghton Mifflin, 1935); and Dianna Everett, *The Texas Cherokees: A People Between Two Fires, 1819–1840* (Norman: University of Oklahoma Press, 1990), are broad accounts of subjects that were very important to Houston from 1836 to 1845.

For many years the standard work on annexation was Justin H. Smith, *The Annexation of Texas* (New York: Baker and Taylor Co., 1911), which presented the story in a totally positive light.

Frederick Merk, *Slavery and the Annexation of Texas* (New York: Knopf, 1972), criticized annexation as a victory for proslavery forces employing propaganda and scare tactics. A broader look at the issue is found in David M. Pletcher, *The Diplomacy of Annexation: Texas, Oregon, and the Mexican War* (Columbia: University of Missouri Press, 1973). William C. Binkley, *The Expansionist Movement in Texas, 1836–1850* (Berkeley: University of California Press, 1925), deals with the issue of Texas's western boundary from independence through annexation and the Compromise of 1850.

Of the many important studies of national politics during the era of Houston's senatorial career, David M. Potter, *The Impending Crisis, 1848–1861* (New York: Harper & Row, 1976), is an excellent survey. Little has been published to provide context on Houston's role in Texas politics from 1846 to 1861. Ernest Wallace, *Texas in Turmoil, 1849–1875* (Austin: Steck-Vaughn, 1965), sketches major developments. Earl W. Fornell, *The Galveston Era: The Texas Crescent on the Eve of Secession* (Austin: University of Texas Press, 1961), is helpful as is Sister Paul of the Cross McGrath, *Political Nativism in Texas, 1825–1860* (Washington, DC: Catholic University of America, 1930). Robert K. Peters, "Texas: Annexation to Secession" (Ph.D. diss., University of Texas, 1977), is an unpublished synthesis of politics during the era. Walter L. Buenger, *Secession and the Union in Texas* (Austin: University of Texas Press, 1984), analyzes the secession crisis in all its complexity.

Index